Personal Magic

Conscious Empowerment through Creativity & Spirit

House of Lit

Create a page of pictures for YOUR book!

Kate and Alexa (Christmas 2010)

Kate on stage (Performing Wellness 2010)

Kate riding the red rocks of Sedona (2010)

Personal Magic

Conscious Empowerment through Creativity & Spirit

by

Kate Hawkes

House of Lit

Published in the United States
by
House of Lit
Dewey, AZ 86327

Illustrations by Alexa Kate Soles

Personal Magic Images 7, 8, and the Chakra image by Kate Hawkes

Cover Photos by Kate Hawkes. Cover Image by Hidesy Images

Cover design by Allisone PrintGraphics, Prescott, Arizona

ISBN-13: 978-1466463554
ISBN-10: 1466463554

Note: This publication is designed to provide accurate and authoritative information in regard to the subject matter covered. It is sold with the understanding that the Publisher is not engaged in rendering professional services. If professional advice or other expert assistance is required, the services of a competent professional should be sought.

TABLE OF CONTENTS

DEDICATION

This book is dedicated to Alexa who from the moment she arrived in my life has been a gift, a treasure, a challenge and a joy. The honor and responsibility of being her Mother impelled me to embrace my personal magic even before I knew that is what I was doing. Thank you.

ACKNOWLEDGMENTS

This book has taken my entire life to come to fruition and there are many to recognize as teachers (often just through shared experiences) and supporters on that journey. Here is a partial list: the students over many years teaching at Linfield College and other workshops and schools; actors, directors, writers and producers in the live theatre world; the writers in the Performing Wellness Workshops; fellow teachers and passionate advocates for the arts; Bonnie Ross, Nurmi Hussa, Colleen Hawkes; and the horses, desert, hot-springs and mountains that sustain me beyond the words and thinking.

PRELUDE

You can be someone who is resilient, optimistic and kind while being realistic in the present world.

You can do this on your own. You don't need a book of tricks, a religion, a guru or a formula. No one becomes a magician by watching magicians. No one can be another person. You *can* be who you are - and that is huge when you truly step right into it.

It is, however, helpful to have a book, a guide, the nudge that keeps saying, "You can do it." No one can walk for you. Only you can walk for yourself, but at times it is helpful to have that *hand* that steadies your hips or holds onto you as your balance slips. Or is offered, as you start up a steep hill, to steady you until your legs are stronger and balance surer. The *voice* of experience that says, as you approach stairs for the first time, "Maybe try it this way."

Most of all though, it is the *cheer squad* that encourages you to rise again when you fall, celebrates the small steps, and honestly admires your journey, that most sustains you.

This little book is that hand, voice and the cheer squad. Nothing is set in stone. Ultimately it is your walking that will take you on your journey.

At first glance this is very simply my story, a culmination of all that I have experienced, read and studied. However, as you read it, it will become your story. It must. Personal Magic is just that – personal - and as such unique to each individual. It is a mighty gift and a big responsibility. What if you were never to try it? What would be missed? What would the world not gain?

I read Viktor Frankel's *The Meaning of Life*. He wrote, "The meaning of life is not in what you get out of it but of what it asks of you." And what is asked of you is that you fulfill your greatest potential, that you experience and manifest your Personal Magic. In the giving is the receiving.

The book you are about to co-create works this way:
I write some ideas I have uncovered for myself, that work for me on the journey to my Personal Magic, and also for some others. I offer you the opportunity and space to try them out

and uncover your story. I am a hand along the way and a cheer squad when you need it on your journey.

So, the first step on your journey:

- While much of the writing/art can be done in this book itself (yes WRITE IN YOUR BOOK!) you will need extra. Have at hand a sheaf of blank 8x11 paper and, of course, a writing implement. Please, please do this. Don't say, "I'll do it later." (Okay, I know it is your journey, but I have been up and down these stairs myself a few times!) I recommend a pen rather than a pencil, so you are not tempted to erase anything. Whatever you write, however it comes out, spelling unusual or regular, non sequitur, unfinished thoughts, run on sentences, is right. There is no need to think about erasing anything! Maybe have two pens in case one runs out or you misplace one.
- You will see at the end of each section is a line (for your name), an 's', and the words 'Personal Magic,' so it would read 'XXXX's Personal Magic' followed by numbers 1, 2, 3, etc.. Following that is a prompt. Simply pick up that pen and write, or draw, or whatever the prompt suggests directly onto the book.
- After each Personal Magic Activity, write a Note To Self. Something like: 'This was interesting because....' Or 'I found out....' Or simply 'Right now I am feeling...' It will be where you step back, comment on the activity and how you relate to it.
- Notice that there is a wide margin on the outside of each page. This is your place to doodle, write comments, drop crumbs, spill coffee or stick your gum. You might also be inspired to illustrate the book here as you read.

A couple more little goodies to have on hand:

- Small box of crayons and/or colored pencils with a sharpener.
- A CD mix of your favorite music as well as those I have suggested at the back of this book. *(Prepare this before you start the book!)*
- Finally, if possible, have a timer handy or at least a watch you can set to beep.

All of these things, this book included, are best kept together in one box or bag so that you pick up the book and everything else comes along as well. These things are your hands along the way and the cheer squad - dancers and all!

You will find out that you know much more than you think you do, and this knowledge is an articulation of your Personal Magic. As you take this journey, you will be accessing the wisdom and support you have within as well as my two cents worth.

And now we can begin.

INTRODUCTION

Personal Magic offers a way of being in the world, a way to live your life with power, resilience, hopefulness and - ultimately - with joy.

Why do I offer it? Why do I think that we need yet another book on self-improvement, empowerment or whatever it is? Because every time I look at the TV or read the paper, I see it plain as day. Because I meet people and hear their stories and know that for too many the loss of a job, a partner, a house, their health leaves them afraid, shattered and most of all, with no sense of *who they are.*

There are the 'reality' TV shows, widespread abuse of our bodies and nationwide denial of those things which are most difficult to contemplate (lack of clean air, water and food). At the least, there seems to be an inability to squarely face our lives and the world in which we live without dissolving into fear, intolerance and/or depression. It is symptomatic of a nation of people who have no center of true Self, no connection to something greater than their own apparently disintegrating universe. Call it no hope, no resilience, no soul even.

There are children so full of fear and rage that they intentionally create fights and video them; adults so lacking in confidence that they crave more and more material goods at the cost of almost everything else; people so empty of joy that they eat themselves into stupors. Others are seeking the quick fix - of their appearance, in their emotional life, for their future - through a diet, a holiday, a religion.

The way out of these dead ends, struggling through the maze of corruption, fear and ignorance and into a future that resounds with wellbeing at all levels, is really quite simple. Simple but not easy. It is not easy only because as a culture we are bereft of the skills to do what is natural for every living being on the planet. We are so separated from those skills that in fact the very thought (for many of us) of accessing what is readily available to each of us is terrifying. Others are willing to step into what they feel is there but often do so out of fear and with a grasping neediness that almost suffocates the access.

INTRODUCTION

What is it that is there for each of us? The intangible but universal Spirit. Call it God, Creator, call it Power, Life itself, call it molecules from the Big Bang, it doesn't matter. Throughout all cultures, in all times and in spite of many efforts to eradicate reference to Spirit, the human simpatico with Spirit persists. And has also done so in spite of the damage done by organized dogma and religion, which over many years has almost strangled the personal relationship between Individual and Spirit.

While a yearning for a connection to Spirit persists, many individuals regardless of their culture, belief system, education (or lack of), and/or socioeconomic status live separated from their own Soul. And when you don't know your Soul you tend to miss out on the Spirit, and so live, lost and fearful, in a constant state of searching and dislocation.

I have wandered through those vast stretches of nowhere-ness a few times myself over the years. I have been afraid, angry, mis-trustful, terribly hurt and betrayed and graspingly needy. Somehow, luckily and by hard work and determination, often with the unwitting support and encouragement of people with whom I worked and played, I have evolved through those challenges. I am stronger, kinder, more generous, compassionate and more able to be wrong, to let go and to allow curiosity to overcome fear.

When the passages of fear, paralysis and neediness arrive in my doorstep, I recognize them more immediately, sweep them away more vigorously and let the experience of that passage inform my knowledge as I move forward. What I have come to know is that I am not here alone and the nowhere-ness is actually a vast ocean of everything-ness when I can connect with its depths openly and consciously. What I always have at my disposal is my Soul and my creative drive.

I offer this little book to you as a means by which you can strenghten your connection to your innermost self, or Soul, and be free of fear. The time IS now. Change is underway, economically, environmentally, and with all that, socially, whether we like it or not.

Of course you are anxious. Old rules are evaporating before your eyes, and the structures and institutions that have supported them are crumbling with widespread ramifications. Do you grab for all you can now? Do you hunt around for a lifeboat on which you can climb aboard and play by those rules? Do you shut the door and medicate yourself out of the picture?

When your life changes in ways that you did not plan or ever dream of, when you are face to face with just your self, when you seem to be all that is left - are you frozen with grief? blinded by blame? panicked into a frenzy of counterproductive action?

Or do you eyeball the opportunity and rise to the challenge to make the Apocalypse before you into what it can truly be. Apocalypse - not just the end, but the necessary cleansing for beginning. We in the West forget that second bit. Forget or have been taught that it is the end of the world - period. We are told that if you wish to be saved then you must believe this, do that, follow these rules. Actually, life goes on regardless of what you do or don't do. The only choice is *how YOU go on* in the midst of change. Things must be shed, burned and

INTRODUCTION

lost before the new can grow. Look at the forest after the bushfire, out of the black earth come those amazing flowers. Remember too that fish emerge out of long-dry lake beds. Returning into life can be gentle, reassuring, powerful and joyful.

This book, *Personal Magic,* is a key to rising from the ashes, to being your own Phoenix. I will not say 'simply rising' because you may have to learn to walk again and then to fly. However, it is a natural way of being through natural means - creating, breathing, taking personal responsibility for your Self and for others. Maybe you have not reached the melting point, in which case this book may help you avoid it altogether. Think of Personal Magic as providing tools of prevention as well as of regeneration.

The greater the challenges, the greater the potential for real change into good health and wellbeing at many levels. The Personal Magic way of Being will impact your relationship with the following areas:
- your own lifestyle, personal relationships and work you do
- illness, death and dying (and thus the healthcare system)
- your ability to handle stress and cope with the changes ahead

Some of the areas this book explores include:
- the spiritual domain
- the arts and creativity
- the arts and healthcare

I write more about this in the first chapter but the spiritual approach that currently works best for myself is the Shamanic paradigm, and the main form of my expression has been through the arts, and theatre in particular. This book has grown out of what I learned through my work in education, theatre, and the arts in healthcare, with the current place in my spiritual journey.

Magic is something you can only practice by doing. You do not become magic by watching a magician. Everyone has their own expression of magic in the world, and you will only experience your true power and joy when you find and live that uniquely *you* magic.

So, this book will offer time and activities for you to begin to know your Personal Magic. It can be two books, mine and yours. You may read the book and ignore the participatory activities, or you might just do the activities. I think that doing the activities without reading the stories behind them will mean that your magic may likely be more rote as you simply follow directions without context. If you read the stories and don't do the exercises then you miss an opportunity to uncover and strengthen *your* Personal Magic, or it will be of a weaker more imitative kind.

Real magic means being able to transform what you hear, read, see, into your own voice and path. Ultimately this book is about finding *your* path, your Spirit's quest if you like. You will have purpose, know why you are here, and uncover the magic that is yours, and only yours, to do and bring into the world.

INTRODUCTION

If we are to not just survive but thrive in the years ahead, we will all need to be aware of and have the courage to manifest our Personal Magic in the world.

I offer this book in the belief that it will assist you in fulfilling your greatest potential - to be a powerful, kind, resilient and confident individual with unique magic to share with the world

CHAPTER ONE – BASIC CONCEPTS

As much as I want to just set off on the trail and up the mountain, I also think a few definitions will be useful. Kind of like checking that you have the necessary items for a hiking trip - backpack, good boots, a hat. So, let's look briefly at the following:

• Spirit/Soul

• Creativity as a Way into Spirit

• Where this Interacts with our Health

These are my definitions, how I understand these concepts and will refer to them in this book. You can write in your 'understandings' as well at the end of each section.

SPIRIT

A little bit of my 'spiritual journey' story may be useful here. I grew up in Australia, attended a Church of England girls boarding school where every school day began with a short service and each evening closed with evening prayers. Sundays we had the full communion service and sometimes I even played the organ for the sung service. Loved that music!

Somehow I never managed to make the commitment to Confirmation in spite of two attempts. It was, even then, too important to me to stand up and publicly announce a faith I did not feel in something as central to the tenet that Jesus Christ rose again on the third day.

Later in the USA I read books by Mathew Fox (*Original Blessing*) and attended a workshop where I learned about 'heretical breathing'. I explored Creation Spirituality and read Charlene Spretnak's *States of Grace*. I wrote a play for children (*Singing Our Way Home*) about the Indigenous Australian people's dreamtime and notion of singing the landscape into being. Delving into that beautiful vision articulating our place on this earth as human beings resonated with me.

I spent a number of years with Buddhism - a gentle, wise and for me very healing way of being. Indeed in many ways, I am still comfortable in that zone, incorporating it casually into my life. I think it is not too far from the Shamanic practice.

Four years ago I landed by roundabout means on the Shamanic paradigm. That view and articulation of how power works, the relationship between soul and body and mind came easily and in many ways is inclusive of what has gone before.

So as I define Spirit here it is rooted in the shamanic understanding but in no way precludes any of the great traditions where human beings attempt to bring to a conscious level their innate and deeply felt connection to something far larger than the human form. Language –

words and concepts - are simply ways of trying to bring something intangible to the mind's surface, transforming it into something tangible by which we can understand our path in this life.

....

Spirit is invisible, intangible and all around. Think of a sound wave without the sound. Spirit is a frequency that when in contact with a specific kind of power will resonate in such a way that its presence (sound) is fully available to the conscious mind. That Power is held in the Soul.

The Soul contains the Life Force or Power necessary for Spirit to transform from that soundless frequency into something that can manifest into tangible everyday reality.

And the instrument that provides the means by which the Frequency (Spirit) and the Power (Soul) can together be seen, heard and felt, is the body/mind consciousness.

Spirit has a path to follow; each Soul with which it comes in contact energizes an aspect of that path, and therefore each instrument has a particular expression of that path to put into the world.

In short, each of us has a part to play in this orchestra of the universe - our own unique melody within the greater symphony. When we play that which is ours to play, we are embraced and enlarged by the whole of which we are part.

PERSONAL MAGIC

If we don't have the music, or don't hear the melody or resist the rhythm, then we have an experience of being outside of ourselves, at odds with the world. How do we hear the melody? Where is the music? It is in Awareness….simply being in the present moment. The rhythm is played out when the Soul interprets the Spirit to us, into our body/mind consciousness.

We are at our most powerful and effective in this life when we are in Awareness of our Soul's connection to Spirit, when we are in tune with the music. And through this awareness we come to know what is our expression in the world (*aka* Spirit's Path, Heart's Desire or Personal Magic). And that is not found in a book but through personal *felt* experience.

For now, suffice to say the degree to which we manifest in the world depends on our degree of Awareness of Spirit. And here is the tricky thing: Awareness, although it requires Consciousness in order for us as human Beings to recognize it as such, is not the same as ego consciousness. The ego exists through analysis and judgment, is emotionally involved and, as such, is reactive.

True, pure Spirit Awareness is simply aware. You can observe, know and be in the is-ness without comment. All that you need is Now. That is, when you are in Awareness you can be Conscious of Spirit as it pertains directly and only to you.

Each of us is an instrument for manifestation or expression. And magically enough, each of us has our own particular shape, or Soul, through which Spirit wishes to express itself. This is not invasion of the body snatchers! Just as the Life Force/Soul contains Power for Spirit's transmutation to 'sound,' so our Soul will only function at its most efficient when aligned with the Spirit. Together this creates a frequency resonant only in that Being. Therefore each human being carries within the urge to live according to Spirit, and each vessel (Soul) is unique. Thus each of us has our own unique magic to perform - our personal Spirit Path in expression of the Great Spirit.

If you can open yourself to the path that is yours, coordinating the Power so freely available within you, with the Frequency all around, you will indeed come into your Personal Magic.

To Recap:

• Spirit is invisible and forever and can be manifest through all natural things.

• We all have a container of Life Force, a Soul, through which Spirit can manifest.

• Each of us is a unique instrument and therefore each of us has a Personal Magic.

• When you manifest that magic, you feel joy and the world around you benefits as well.

_____'s Personal Magic 1

Take a breath, close your eyes, feel and hear your heart
beating.
Listen for about a minute. What is your tune?

Write or draw whatever comes to you. Resist thinking or
understanding, expanding or explaining, just scribble with
words or shapes and lines for 5 minutes (set the timer).

(Note To Self...)

CREATIVITY AS A WAY INTO SPIRIT

Have you ever watched a small child engrossed in painting?
Have you suddenly written a poem? Found yourself humming
a melody you have never heard before? Free-danced on your
own? When you are in those states, unconscious of the
physical world around you, letting intuition and the power of
the moment guide you, not planning an outcome, nor
criticizing the creation as it unfolds, you are functioning in
Spirit. You are in Awareness and of that moment, not in the
past or the future but Now.

'The Spirit of creativity,' 'the creative Spirit,' 'a free Spirit.' It
is no accident that these phrases abound. When you are in that
creative inner world, you are indeed at your most free because
that is where we make contact with the Spirit that moves
through us. It is where you are free of the rules, expectations

inhibitions, and anxieties of being 'right' and 'successful.' It is where you will truly create and clearly develop awareness of something you did not *know*.

People who create great art, those who invent things, and those who 'see' solutions to impossible problems with leaps of understanding that open up an entirely new field of knowing (such as quantum physics) have not opened those doors by sitting down and working it out. They may have started there - think of that as 'technique' - but the aha!, the magic, happened when they relaxed into the moment of discovery, putting aside rational rules and expectations. This makes room for that unknown way of KNOW-ing (or Awareness) to move into the void. The Void is that space between the vast inadequacy of what we *know* consciously and the effort to force an outcome.

There is so much more than we *know* beneath the layer of everyday consciousness by which we usually operate in the world. The creative Spirit frees us to access the deeper, richer KNOW-ledge beyond mere rational, learned thought and knowledge. In short, we are simply and purely in Awareness. We are not thinking.

Mindfulness, meditation, in the flow… It is not so much about changing *what is* as it is about adjusting how we perceive it, understand it, experience it. It is a transmutation of experience from one level to another. It is magic.

PERSONAL MAGIC

The ancient practice of Shamanism takes us, with intention, into that inner world. For as long as human beings have been on earth, shamanic practices to maximize human abilities of mind and spirit for healing have been practiced. Essentially, the shamanic approach uses breathing techniques, combined with a willingness to draw on the natural power sources around you, dream-time and letting go of outcome. Choosing to enter into this other way of KNOW-ing, this Awareness, is not a prayer for an answer to some problem, but more like opening a door and seeing what is there without judgment or even expectation.

The creative endeavor of making art, expressing yourself artistically, or simply listening and paying attention to another's expression of art so much so that you become drawn into that sphere of consciousness, also takes you beyond the rational mind. It takes you through the doorway of your Soul into Spirit, and the visions, ideas, sudden 'ahas!' that emerge are not from your mind, but your Spirit. It is also from there you can create art. The very same way you entered is also the way to give expression to that experience.

Yes, it is circular. You put yourself into a creative state to create. You put yourself into a state that opens you to Spirit to encounter Spirit. You have to use magic to find magic. The physical expression of that encounter in the visible world is your Personal Magic made manifest. And that is what this book will help you to do.

To Recap:

- The mental/emotional state we are in when engaged in creative endeavor opens up access to a different level of Awareness and understanding than the usual rational daily consciousness.
- It is possible to choose to enter that state through a range of activities.
- In Shamanic terms, we have conscious access to our Soul and Spirit that flows through our Being.

_____'s Personal Magic 2

Have one of those blank pieces of paper handy. Name it (your name) Personal Magic #2.

Put in your CD, selecting a track that has no words.

Take a couple of deep breaths, relax your shoulders, listen to the music.

When the track ends, put it on again.

This time while the music plays, with the crayons/pencils draw, color, noodle in on the entire blank page - just shapes, line and color. (You want to add a few single words as well.)

When the track ends, if you need to, play it one more time and keep drawing/writing.

When the track ends this time, stop. You are done.

Take a moment to really look at your creation with open eyes and heart, as if you have never seen it before!

(Note To Self...)

_____'s Personal Magic 3

Now, without thinking too hard, in the space below, write quickly and simply your understanding of Spirit and Soul. You may want to write a short spiritual journey narrative, or you may simply want to draw images and/or just color and shapes.

(Note To Self...) *(remember this is an opportunity to comment on the exercise form the 'outside' as it were.)*

WHERE THIS INTERACTS WITH OUR HEALTH

And what has this to do with health?

Shamanism is a cultural practice that engages us in Spirit. Traditionally the Shaman was a healer and also a specialist in the soul, that intermediary between our Body/Mind Consciousness and Spirit. Early cultures believed that illness was closely related to Spiritual causes and a powerful way to understand that relationship was through artistic expression or storytelling. Telling the story gave it expression, and in doing so transformed the experience. (*Magic....*)

Some examples of how the arts and healing interacted are found in Egyptian and Sumerian art, sacred art and sacred healing in the Judaic, Christian and Buddhist traditions, Tibetan Buddhist art, Native American and Celtic cultures, the Australian Aboriginal Dreamtime, and Aztec and Toltec traditions. (It is both ancient and pervasive through all indigenous cultures and times.)

As human culture evolved and changed, so specialists became more specialized. There were artists and there were healers, and the people went to those specialists to have their needs met in those areas. Often they were included very directly in ceremonies to effect their healing, and there were festivals and opportunities for the entire community to participate in group activities addressing sudden events, specific needs and long-term plans for the 'health' of the society.

These were generally led by the Shaman, were public andeveryone had a role. The Shaman was also, if not the Spiritual leader, still working closely to bring into being a Spiritual life for the community. The Shaman was also often the 'medicine man/woman' and recognized healer who actively engaged the person seeking healing in a personal and individual process.

Over time, further separation occurred and there were fewer opportunities for participatory public ritual (large crowds watched the specialists!); arts became something most of us didn't make/create but bought from the specialist; and the healer became the doctor. He didn't ask us to participate so much as gave us things to take (note 'to take' not 'to do') *and* did things *to* us. And the Spirituality of the community became an organized religion and was also administered by those who *knew* and interpreted those laws. The majority of us became passive recipients, not creators or doers, of the care and knowledge concerning our physical and Spiritual health.

Most recently on this continuum of 'development,' as knowledge of the physical dimensions of the body grew and healing became affiliated with science, so the arts somehow had nothing at all to do with health any more. The exception was that in times of natural disasters or traumatic events, the community would come together to share the experience through music and art. It was a spontaneous convergence, a primal urge to connect, to somehow converse about the trauma through a form that was not intellectual or through everyday consciousness, but through that place within, beyond the rational.

The good news is that the 'development' continuum is not a straight line heading nowhere. It is actually circular or maybe spiral, like a staircase rising up and circling through phases that we can recognize when we look back. And, like a spiral staircase heading upwards, one we can build upon. So it is not surprising to me that it is now common for the medical world to speak of the body/mind connection and even, sometimes, the body/mind/spirit connection. There is Patient Centered Medicine where the person with the illness or trauma is invited to tell the story of that illness, and their participation is considered essential to healing and wellness. Participation is also recognized as essential for a peaceful death.

In these times of great change with inevitable loss, fear and simply not 'knowing' what to do next, the body/mind/spirit connection is a useful means of engaging in your healing. When you are your own healer, not only do you access your power, you are also contributing to the community, the nation and the world. Bring your Personal Magic to the table, be at the center of your story, as a creator, not a victim, and connect with the Shaman within.

After so many generations of cultural disconnect from your own sense of power and from your Awareness of Self - from, in short, your Spirit - it is hardly surprising that the thought of becoming central to your story is often overwhelming. "How do I do it? What if I screw it up?"

It is also, though, alluring, and you lean into the possibility of once again being whole and powerful. Sometimes you say to yourself or to your doctor, "I KNOW this is what is happening.' You can't say where that came from, but it *feels* right.

That is your Spirit whispering, "Yes, me." And when you Pay Attention, when you Act on that whisper, you will feel a surge of power and joy.

This is not to say you should rush about telling everyone what to do, and just pleasing yourself. In fact, if you were to do that it would indicate that you had quite lost touch with Spirit and were simply letting your ego run rampant with some new gizmo. The practice of real Personal Magic requires responsibility, courage and discipline.

To Recap:
- When we participate in the story of our life we become healers in our personal world.
- Healing is related to Spirit. It is possible to transmute that experience of illness into something life-affirming, and the arts are a means by which we can accomplish that.
- Transformation is magical and that power carries with it responsibility and has capacity to positively affect the world around us.

_____'s Personal Magic 4

On one of the blank pieces of paper, write (your name)
Personal Magic 4.

Draw a simple stick figure, in the middle of the page with
about 2 inches above and below.

Breathe deeply, relax your body and mind.

Recall a time when you were helpless, either sick or unable
to physically achieve something you wanted to do, or when
someone was particularly unkind to you and you took it
with no response.

(Keep it short: one interaction or attempt, 30 minutes span
in real time max.)

Where were you?

Who was there?

What colors, sounds, shapes, smells, textures?

Replay the event to the moment when you realized that
you could not effect the change/impact that you wanted.

Now, stop the 'tape' right there....

Get out the pen, and on the back of the drawing page, write
a version where you say what you wanted to say, find that
extra inch, strength, or the illness evaporates.

In short, you are as powerful as you wish you had been.

See yourself as this powerful person. HOWEVER, the
power is not emanating from the outside, but from the
_in_side.

Return to the stick figure you drew earlier. Using the colors you have, draw/indicate the magic exuding <u>from</u> that stick figure, the power radiating out to all around.

Add smaller stick figures of others (people or objects) in your story. Put them on the outer edges of the page - you are in the center.

Add more colors, lines and circles, emanating from the central stick figures' heart (yours) to touch all others around.

With more colors, expand the outline and shape of that central stick figure, by tracing it just beyond it current lines, and then again and again, until it becomes big and colorful. It will be less a stick figure, with more layers and layers, until it is almost 3-D.

See the transformation from thin stick figure to colorful layered work of art in the center of the page touching all around you. In this picture, what you didn't do or say, couldn't do or make happen is no longer material. That figure at the center radiates beauty and power regardless of the story.

Write your name above that Being, and breathe into being the healer at the center of the page.

(Note To Self...)

This book will assist you to both find your real magic and to develop the skills and understanding to respect that magic. You can then choose to use it wisely and for the good of your Spirit, those around you and all living beings that you have never met. In this way, the principals of the Shamanic arts (Spirit), the creative arts, and healing in everyday life will positively contribute to your health and wellbeing. It will also radiate out to other individuals, communities and environments as well as The Planet and her Universe.

A Word on Magic

Real magic is not illusion. That is sleight of hand. I am talking about actually transmuting something, changing it from one 'thing' to another - alchemy.

Shamanism is an earth-based wisdom rooted in the concept that we are all a part of the power-full forces of nature. Magic is not an invisible intangible, but the observable outcomes of your behavior. When you reach into your Soul, through the Heart, and listen to your Spirit's truth, you are indeed magic and powerful. There are physical 'things you can do' to open up that space, but there is no one way and no one can do it for you. Your magic and your power are not handed to you, and do not depend on a guru or priest to manifest. It is solely your creation.

Investigate and experience a range of opportunities to open up your heart, blend the intellect with intuition, create ritual and rhythm in your life. Ultimately, how that is for you, how that magic works for you, is yours. *There* is the power, arising within your Being, expressed in the world.

A Word about Joy

This is a word used in Christian, Sufi and Shamanic circles. It is really a very straightforward experience due to simple direct causes. It is that directly FELT experience, when you have forgotten your emotional, physical self, and are fully involved in the moment, whatever it is. It is not about comfort or safety or even peace. It is being absolutely with/in where you are. In short, those moments when you are directly in tune with your Spirit, with God, with Creator. Gratitude, oneness, purpose, power, and meaning. Joy.

This book includes ways in which the arts, and specifically writing, open you to that experience and power. Too often we are enmeshed in the intellect - thinking, problem solving, planning, fixing the past. The arts simply say 'It is this now.' As an artist we move beyond understanding (philosophy) and illness (healing) and become gift-givers. The journey may (and probably will) involve the other aspects, but in the end you are the creator of your life. The act of creation transmutes fear and helplessness into courage and power. Magic indeed. YOU are the alchemist, and no matter how many assist you on the way, the ultimate magic arises in you. Now you are truly empowered.

CHAPTER TWO – AWARENESS OF SELF

When we are young, very young (and for some of us that wild, free child lasts longer), we enter into the creative moment so easily. The line between conscious everyday reality and that great inner world - alternative or deeper  consciousness - is more fluid. Children play, draw, dance, sing, wonder and dream with no self-consciousness. By that I mean that they are not uncomfortable with who they are - nor, therefore, with what they create and imagine.

The concept of 'self' is essential to this book and the expression of Personal Magic. Much has been written about 'self' within the context of the philosophical and psychological, religious and sociological, the personal and cultural.

Very simply, I summarize three main stages in the maturing of 'Self' in human beings within society and culture. First the baby becomes aware that there is him/her (Self), with other objects and beings beyond its own flesh. (Who knows? Maybe at this stage a baby is also aware of beings even beyond the everyday reality?) At this stage the baby/young child has no notion of being right or wrong, or needing to fit into a certain form or framework. Indeed, the very young child seems to be curious and accepting of almost any person or object that comes into view, touch, taste or smell.

In the second stage, human beings become self-conscious; that is, he/she begins to see him/herself in comparison to others, to judge and evaluate his/her own Self in relation to the other human beings in the immediate and then the larger community and the world.

It is at that stage that most young people begin to lose that connection with the deeper inner world, with their Personal Magic. Some may appear to go deeper into the realm for periods of time, and some may not be able to connect at all with our everyday reality. I will come back to this. Sufficient for now to suggest that when you go deeply into your inner consciousness without being able to consciously move back again, then you are not in your Personal Magic but in a place that is an escape *from y*ourself. Personal Magic requires that you connect deeply with both your inner world <u>and</u> the outside earth-world. It is not a means of hiding.

A Useful Diversion

Even I get a little muddled with all the different interpretations of Unconscious and   Conscious. So to clarify, in this book, this is how I am using those terms.

There is being unconscious in the sense of being physiologically inert to physical stimulation (*i.e.*, asleep, in a coma). And there is being Unconscious in the sense of being unaware of all the levels and means by which you operate. Thus, you tend to simply react - often without knowing you are, let alone why, and choosing a response. I will be using the term in this sense unless I say otherwise.

There is being conscious physiologically; you hear people talking to you, you feel hot and cold etc. And there is being Conscious in the spiritual/intellectual sense when you know who you are and how you operate in the world. Thus, you *make choices* and *respond* to situations, people and life itself. It is this meaning to which I am referring unless otherwise stated.

The third stage of Self, which is not a given as are the other two, is Awareness of Self. Somehow there is another Being in the room - not just *my*-self and the *other*-selfs, by whom I live in comparison, but an objective, removed-from-the-fray-of-everyday-life Being. Your level of consciousness has taken a quantum leap forward in this stage! You are operating from the place of the Higher Self, or Spirit.

It is actually Awareness of Spirit. It may sound paradoxical, but think about it - we are all Spirit, and it is through Spirit that we have Awareness of Self!

AND the creative endeavor gets you there, plus the art you create in that mode is the purest expression of that Awareness of Self.

So on my continuum, that is the third stage of 'self' in human development - Awareness of Self - and that is manifest through our Personal Magic. Unfortunately, we can get stuck before we arrive there, or we visit in short intermittent bursts.

But before we go there, it is time for another chapter in *your* book.

_____'s Personal Magic 5

Stage 1) Barely self aware

Think of babies you have observed or known. Remember how surprised they can be to see something can leave their hand and appear somewhere else, or their focus on something moving in the air (a mobile), or how they can simply suck their entire fists while singing to themselves. We have all seen the look of concentration and then contentment that comes over their face with a bowel movement and heard the unabashed vocal expressions that accompanies hunger, pain or fear.

It is best to do this exercise when you can be sure that you will not be interrupted so that you can completely relax and DO it fully!
Read all the directions first and then just jump in. Don't worry if you forget something.

Make yourself comfortable on the floor, or a bed, so that you are lying prone. In that position, close your eyes and take 3 deep breaths.

Breath 1: Relax your body, allow your knees to fall outward, your stomach to relax and your jaw sag.

Breath 2: Feel where you are touching the surface upon which you are lying. Note the texture, the temperature, the flexibility of it as it relates to your body weight and shape.

Breathe 3: Bring your hands together, facing up, resting your wrists on your stomach, fingers open, palm to palm and press them together.

In that position, still breathing, listen to everything that you can hear outside of the room. Notice the sounds, identify them, then let them go.

After a while, listen to everything in the room that you are in. Identify, let go.

Now listen to your own sounds - your heart-beat, breath and your blood moving through your body.

Next, with your eyes still closed, feel everything that you can around you - your clothes, the surface on which you are lying, your own skin and body. Really feel it - run your fingers lightly over the surface then gradually press harder. Notice taste in your mouth, on your hand, etc.

What can you smell? Your clothes, your hair, the paper etc.

Open your eyes. Sit up and really look at the room - colors, shapes - and look for a minute detail. When you see that detail, (it might be a crack, a dirty mark, a speck of paper) investigate it even more closely. With all your senses, get to know it. (Take about 2 minutes for this.)

Lie back down again, close your eyes, place your hands together, palm to palm as they were, breathe deeply back into your body, and return your focus back on your inner world. Let the detail go completely.

Take one final deep breath, expel it suddenly and completely, before opening your eyes and sitting up again.

You just had an experience of being completely in your own inner world, then connecting to the outside one as if never seeing it before. You randomly selected and investigated one detail that has no personal meaning to you, before fully letting it go and returning to your world.

Babies do this all the time - even *with* an audience. It is a very free to place to be.

Stage 2) Self conscious

Think of someone whose good opinion you would like to have. It may be a family member, co-worker, or someone else you'd like to impress.
Get a clear image of that person.
Stand in your room.
Place that person, in your minds eye, opposite you in the room.
Now, from where you have placed them, look back at yourself.
Notice what you are wearing, color, texture, shape and how it looks on you.
From that other person's position in the room, look at your hair, hands and feet.

Take a moment and notice how you feel.

How is it different to the previous exercise?
Is one more relaxing than the other?
Take a deep breath, expel it quickly and release any
tension or anxiety.

Take a little (5 mins.) time to write your experience of the
two exercises. Brief description of what you saw, how you
felt during each and after each.

(Note To Self...)

SELF-AWARENESS or AWARENESS OF SELF?

Many people work hard on self-awareness. They want to be aware of their emotions, beliefs, attitudes, modes of communication and deep-seated fears. Self-awareness implies being self-conscious, having an identity. Identity is generally a pretty static thing. 'This is who I am, how I live, what I believe and what I give and do in the world.' It is closely associated with ego. If that self-awareness is fraught with anxiety at what you see, then you can be crippled with embarrassment or shyness. And sometimes that self-awareness, anxiously competing for a place in the world, exhibits itself as brash, overbearing, loud and selfish.

Time for a Word on the Ego

As I am using it in this book, ego is this: The foot soldier of the earth-conscious self, the aspect that works to ensure that you are safe, happy and secure in this earthly realm. The ego is not a bad thing unless it is allowed to be in charge and run the entire show.

You hope to be objective in your self-awareness and know yourself honestly. The problem with that is your evaluative measures are generated from Self. The tools of evaluation are those by which you have built the self-awareness. (The student setting and grading the paper.) Standing in the center of your self you fashion a self and then evaluate that self. The entire focus is both from and to that ego-ic center, the self. A self-generated and re-generating closed circle.

There is nothing inherently wrong with cultivating self-awareness, just as there is nothing inherently wrong with the ego, but it is only a step on the road to really knowing who you are. If you get stuck there, self-awareness begins to stagnate and perhaps even to rot....

What if you turn the words around? Awareness of Self. That implies that there is an outside observer to the Self, one that is aware of it without being *inside* or *of* it. Awareness of Self conjures up an image of something greater than the Self, that can therefore know the Self more objectively than mere self-awareness. When you are Aware of Self you are not inside the experience or defined by it, and thus can accept what you see without arrogance or editing, justification or apology.

Living in Awareness of Self you will never be embarrassed or shy, nor overbearing and controlling. Your ego will have no place to impose its will although you will be aware of those concerns and needs. This is because that ego is part of the circle of which you are aware - and not dictating the circle and whom is doing what within it. The Acting Ringmaster has ended up on the edges of the circle, and is not holding the whip!

HOW TO GET THERE FROM HERE

How do you attain that Awareness of Self? A first step is to access Nonattachment. Now stay with me on this. Reading through this concept, particularly if it new to you, can be a bit like wading knee-deep through ocean waves. The current pulls you one way, your legs push the other against the water, and once in a while a wave splashes you in the face. But it is worth it! When this muscle gets through the first workout it becomes easier and easier from then on.

Read slowly with your pencil in hand. Make notes, doodle and rewrite in your words as you go. So, here goes!

Attachment - Nonattachment - detachment. This looks like a continuum but is actually a circle. Bend the line around to where it connects and you will see that attachment and detachment are the same. One expresses itself by *adhering to* and the other by *separating from*. Whether 'attached' nor 'nonattached' each relationship is inextricably binding and affects your personal expression and being in the world.

Even if you seal yourself into detachment (that is, shut the emotions and feelings away), you are still attached to the 'drama,' the remembered emotion, the history, whatever it is from which you are working so hard to detach. That effort comes from being attached to it, and by that I mean thinking it matters somehow, that it defines you, letting it/fearing it will hurt you.

Nonattachment removes that binding so that you will know there is one Being there and another here, and how each expresses itself in the world is not dependent upon the other. You still interact, and experience emotion and feeling between and within relationship. However, because you can access Nonattachment, you can appreciate yourself as a complete, separate Being, not dependent on others for your sense of self. You can also therefore appreciate others as such.

(I have written in terms of people, but this also includes experiences, possessions, status. And each of these are - when all is said and done - tied up with relationship to others.)

I considered the word 'neutral' as a synonym for Nonattachment, but it doesn't feel right. Neutral is the car out of gear but still running waiting to speed forward or reverse. As such, it is burning energy and polluting the atmosphere. Nonattachment is simply sitting still with no need or expectation of going anywhere.

In Nonattachment it is easier to place emotions and histories into the 'not about me' basket. Much of the charge you feel is old stuff, and usually very little of what comes at you is about you. When you engage in the struggle, or work hard to deflect it - let alone take it on - you validate it, actually give it life!

When you are truly able to be in Nonattachment you can see the story and not be drowned in it. In Nonattachment, you can say, "That is the story, the drama, this is what I am feeling. However, I am not caught in it. I can choose what to do with this."

If it is something that has 'happened to you,' one thing you can do is to quietly give it back. Not with anger, frustration or resentment (that is attachment!), but with compassion. Compassion, no blame, no intention to harm - simply 'This is yours. I am sorry that you have to carry it about but it is not mine to take on or to fix or even to fight you on.'

(Responding with compassion rather than hate or other intentions to wound or punish will do you no harm. However, the force of negative energy generated by hate or similar emotion, whether you keep it to yourself or vent it, is often more damaging to the one who generates it. It is like eating too many beans or trail mix and giving yourself gas - you feel very uncomfortable and you can't blame the food, because you chose to eat it!)

When you are truly in Nonattachment you are also able to hear a truth or fact about yourself without reacting defensively or emotionally. The 'news' becomes simply that, and not an attack or definition or hard and fast fact. You will know a truth when you hear it, if you are in Nonattachment. And then you choose what to do with that. You can say, "Thank you for that insight. I knew that but hadn't heard it like that before." Or maybe you will say, "I knew that but hadn't realized it *consciously* before now."

You will know the truth when you hear it because you already knew it but were just not aware/conscious of it. In short, when in Nonattachment, you can be compassionate to both the bearer of the news as well as to yourself, the recipient of the news!

_____'s Personal Magic 6

Nonattachment

Think of a time when you were in a disagreement with someone, when you

felt as if you had to defend yourself and had to win and as if not getting the other person to agree to your point of view would mean you had somehow failed.

At the top of an 8x11 sheet of blank paper, draw a 3" diameter circle

Draw one next to it that overlaps by a good inch.

Name each circle by the characters in the Drama (your name and....)

Write the story of the drama. Beginning at top of the left-hand circle, write across the two circles, on through the overlapping area in the middle, left to right, and on down to the bottom of the two circles. Write only *inside* the circles and by all means fill them up.

The story is: Where did this take place? What did you want? What the Other want? What were the key things said to you that you felt you had to defend?

Fully color <u>Your</u> circle one color and the <u>Other</u> circle another, over the writing and all.

Notice the muddy color where the two overlap.

Also, it is now probably hard to read the story, to see where one story begins and other ends.

PERSONAL MAGIC

This is what Attachment is like.

Now take a black magic marker. Draw around the edge of *your* circle again, clearly separating your circle from the other. Get an eraser and try to erase the muddy color and words in the overlapping middle section.

It will still be there in some form and part of your story has also disappeared, and in fact part if it has been left out altogether because it is in other's circle.

This is what Detachment is like. You are still hooked into the other's drama even though you have tried to separate yourself.

Drop down a couple of inches to the middle of the page. Draw a new 3" diameter circle to the left, below the center line of the page. Draw another circle a few inches to the right of that one, not overlapping at all.

Name one circle for your name and the other for the Other in the story. Write in your circle what you want. Write in the other circle what they want. In the space between the circles write where this happened. In lines that might reach outside of the other's circle but not touch yours, write the things the Other said that you felt needed to be defended. Notice how they no longer muddy your circle, how they are separate from you.

In your reply, the same thing. Write an answer that is begun within your circle, might reach out of it, but not invade the other circle.

Notice how the dialogue taking place is now separate, overlapping in the space between, organized and visible. (You do not have to resolve this now – a few lines back and forth will do!)

Color Your circle one color and the Other circle another. While some of the words maybe covered over the story is still pretty clear.

This is what non-attachment looks like.

Look at the two pictures,

How do they *Feel* different as you look at them?

Which do you prefer?

Imagine this can apply not just to relationships but also how you respond with regard to events in your life.

(Note To Self...)

It makes sense to think of attachment/detachment as related to self-awareness and the conscious ego, and Nonattachment as related to Awareness of Self and to a greater or higher power. Awareness of Self is just that: a consciousness that comes from something larger than self, unlike self-awareness, that repeating little circle.

What is this something higher? It is of course Spirit. And you get there through your Soul, the intermediary between ego-ic self and Spirit. Your Soul enables you to have conscious awareness of Spirit's path, and also to have true Awareness of Self. You can be *conscious* of the higher/greater power without losing your Nonattachment or Awareness of Self. Indeed, you have to be in Nonattachment. They are practically the same thing, just a slightly different focus.

So where are your mind and your thoughts in all this? Your mind, with its thoughts based on experiences and intellectual knowledge, makes projections arising from that particular level of consciousness. It can act like a filter blocking access to other forms of knowledge and experiences, such as Awareness of Self. You do need your mind to assist in interpreting the experience/knowledge you can gain through Higher Consciousness, but only in the service of that knowledge and not as a gatekeeper.

When your mind selects the experience for you, then the ego is in charge. When your mind gets sidetracked into stories about who did what to you and why and what that means and what you have to DO about it, you are suddenly back in Self-Awareness and dangerously close to Self-Consciousness.

Remember, get the news and then *make choices* about what to do. Miss that step, and you risk jumping into a very deep rough sea without a life jacket.

This doesn't mean that there are not times when you will respond very quickly and instinctively. Instinctively - that is, from your gut, your Soul, no thinking required. The clearer and more established you are in your Higher Self the faster and more appropriate those responses will be.

Attachment to what you know already (fears, judgment, and self-consciousness as you worry about 'doing it right') prevents greater possibilities. Nonattachment, openness to whatever comes, unanchored by what you already know, with Awareness of Self to simply observe when and how you access (or not) that opportunity, enables expansion of Being.

Looking at it another way, without access to Higher Consciousness/Spirit, you are operating and living in a half-awake-half-conscious state of being. You might feel awake and conscious, especially if you have an active and curious mind, *until* you begin to really explore that universe beyond those small parameters of self-awareness and attachment/detachment. When you enter into the realm of awareness beyond the daily reality, you will be truly awake.

Here is a paradox:
The more Aware of Self you are, the free-er you are to be *with* and *in* the world around you. You have nothing to prove. You observe yourself and others, from outside the inner mechanisms, with no judgment, just with awareness and choices. Your interactions are clear of competition with others or yourself. Conversely, the more Self-Aware

you are, the more you have to keep a close watch yourself, like a jailer rather than a kindly Aunt. The more you have to keep proving yourself. It is a struggle that continually drags other people into your drama. Your constant inner watching of yourself requires others to validate the outcome.

So don't get stuck in self-awareness. It is a nice tool for moving right along into Awareness of Self, like knowing the letters of the alphabet is very nice, but until you can make them into poetry they are almost meaningless.

In order to uncover your Personal Magic, being wide awake will be of enormous benefit. Practice Nonattachment, cultivate Awareness of Self, and the doors to Spirit and thus your Personal Magic will open more readily and with greater clarity.

To Recap:

- Consciousness is the state of being aware of how you are in the world and in connection with your Spirit.
- Awareness of Self is the Higher Consciousness being able to see and know the big picture, without being caught up in the emotional drama of it.
- Nonattachment - the state we are in when we are not caught in the drama. We have nothing to prove, win, defend, get or make happen. So we can pay attention to the entire interaction because we are not blocking or manipulating the material.

Which comes first? They go together, hand in hand, each nurturing and supporting the other. And they together open the door to and nurture your Personal Magic.

_____'s Personal Magic 7

stage 3) - Nonattachment-Awareness of Self

You will need a full sheet of that blank paper. Write your name and Personal Magic 7 at the top.

Drawn a rectangle near the top of the page, about 5 inches long and 2 high.

Draw row of little circles (1/4 inch in diameter), side by side in a line across the page just beneath that rectangle.

Draw 2 wavy lines, one under the other, across the page, about 1 inch below the row of little circles.

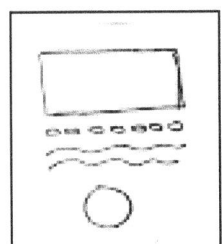 Draw a 3inch diameter circle about 2 inches below the wavy lines.

The top rectangle is a movie screen, the little circles the 'audience' watching it, and the wavy lines are the ocean.

The circle is the sun shining serenely and untouched in the middle.

Name that center sun with *your* name. You are the Sun or Spirit, the Higher Self.

PERSONAL MAGIC

On the movie screen write a list of people, events, issues that really bug you, that (as they say) push your buttons!

Each little head is an aspect of you – your mind, emotions, projections, memories, knowledge. Perhaps place a name on each of these as it relates to the list on the screen. This is your self awareness.

The ocean is your Soul, the means by which you can access that Spirit, that Awareness of Self - the sun.

From each little head draw a wavy line wiggling its way to the ocean/Soul.

Or you can also draw a line from the ocean reaching up to connect to each little head!

Either way, make the direct connection between the mind/body and soul.

NOW, beginning at the <u>bottom</u> of the Sun/Spirit circle, expand that circle upward and round to encompass the waves, the head and at least the bottom of the screen.

There you are! Non-attachment and Awareness of Self, the ability to see the whole story without being defined or swallowed by it.

(Note To Self...)

CHAPTER THREE-EMPOWERMENT

MEET EMPOWERMENT!

Empowerment! What a heady word! But it is a logical extension of Awareness of Self and Personal Magic's twin. I took a  look at the two little dictionaries that live on my desk and came up with this.

From the *Oxford English Dictionary*: empower - authorize (to do); enable.

And from *Random House*: empower - to give power or authority to; to enable or permit.

And then of course, I had to Google (and there are a zillion entries there!).

And I gained this from Wikipedia *(underline mine)*: 'Empowerment refers to increasing the spiritual, political, social or economic strength of individuals and communities. <u>It often involves the empowered developing confidence in their own capacities.</u>

And in particular under Personal Development: 'In the arena of personal development, empowerment forms an apogee of many a system of self-realization or of identity (re-) formation. Realizing the solipsistic impracticality of everyone anarchistically attempting to exercise power over everyone else, empowerment advocates have adopted the word "empowerment" to offer the attractions of such power, but they generally constrain its individual exercise to potentiality and to feel-good uses within the individual psyche.'

And further *(italics mine)*: 'Empowerment can be attained through one of many ways. An important factor in the discovery and application of the human "*self empowerment*" (*) lies within *the tools used to unveil the truth.*' (**)

And then, because it can often be a revealing excursion, I looked up synonyms and found: grant, <u>authorize</u>, permit, <u>sanction</u>, license, commission, delegate, warrant, dispute, commit, <u>entrust</u>, appoint, approve, countenance, allow, <u>ratify</u>. (I have underlined the ones that most connect with this writing.)

There are two phrases that I want you to consider before we go on with Empowerment.
The first is the use of the phrase * '*Self-Empowerment.*' It is disconcertingly like Self-Awareness.

It is pretty easy to take that surface hit of being egoically powerful because we live in a culture that has for so long been built upon gratification of immediate material desires (not even needs). We tend to recognize the powerful, *self-empowered*, as those who get their physical desires manifest in a tangible world.

The self in this definition is that small self of self-awareness. In general our understanding of Self has been shrunk into a small circling spinning spot - the ego at its most rampant –

with only one concern: to make sure that the fears and discomforts of daily life are covered over.

As you now know, when instead we conceive of Self as being an aspect of something far larger and more entire than we can ever imagine, we have stepped into Awareness of Self.

It requires letting go of having to know exactly where and how you fit and to just accept that you do fit. This is of course very frightening when we always want to KNOW the outcome and dislike ambiguity and fear being wrong. (I will write more on this in the next chapter.) It also requires that you accept that the power and strength of each of us lies not in pulling inward and taking care of only me but rather in reaching out and connecting with others.

I have this image of each us trying to live in a private little house surrounded by a fence. Inside the fence you are in charge. You decide. (Except that you are *held* inside, dependent on others to come to you, confined/defined by your fears and doubts.) Outside the fence there are other considerations, and things can easily get out of your 'control.'

(This might be a good place for a little illustration in the wide margin!)

However, if you need something for your little house, you often have to go beyond the fence. Often when you meet those who can help you with your house and garden, then your place becomes richer, more diverse. When you go to others' homes and gardens, then you are also expanded.

Likewise, if you invite others into your garden, you will be giving them something as well.

This 'power' you have is only power when it turns itself outward rather than serving the narrow ego purpose. Lacking Awareness of Self, the ability to see yourself from a perspective outside of self, in the context of the world and beyond, you remain small and actually powerless. You are trapped in the spinning top of self.

Self-awareness means that you are on the inside, feeling your emotions, skin and mental gymnastics only within the context of your little house. Awareness of Self takes you outside of house and garden, and in so doing, you become more powerful and greater than when you hide indoors.

It is a little quibble, but it's an example of language and how that can shape a belief. Wikipedia's phrase (*) *'application of the human "self empowerment"'* (which was already standing uncomfortably in quotation marks) certainly begged for some clarification. Turn the words around - *Empowerment of Self.* Doesn't that sound and, more importantly, feel better? Empower that larger Self that is beyond competition, need and fear. As you uncover and manifest your Personal Magic, that is the Self that will be empowered and empowering.

Take a moment and look back at Chapter 1, and right under Spirit is a single sentence on Soul. *'The Soul contains the Life Force or Power necessary for Spirit to transform....'* Your power, that which empowers you, is your Soul. And right there is your Personal Magic.

Personal Magic releases you from the confined and confining space, but if you keep it to yourself, that magic may atrophy for want of sustenance from that which is beyond the self. Remember the Soul is a direct connection to Spirit, and Spirit is all around and from/for/to all beings and the world in which they live.

In this way you will not be tempted to '*anarchistically attempt(ing) to exercise power over everyone else*' as Wikipedia so delightfully put it!

The other phrase that stands out to me is (**) '*the tools used to unveil the truth.*' The tools you can draw on are many and varied. The most potent is the wisdom you have within, accessed through your Soul, the arts and through discipline with joy. Creating your Personal Magic book is also one of the tools to unveil the truth, by opening the way to your inner wisdom.

_____'s Personal Magic 8

Imagine that you are standing on the edge of a very high cliff. Behind you is a wide green field and beyond that a neatly laid out village. Beyond that chaos and horror, from which you may have escaped but which in any case you are certain is about to engulf you.

An endless sky rises above you speckled with potential monsoon clouds. Below your next step is a sheer drop over into which you cannot see, even lying on your stomach and craning your head over the edge. It is too steep and too far down. In front of you, on the other side of the chasm, far off in the distance seems to be another land mass with mountains poking up into the sky. Can you see them reaching up?

What will you do?

On a blank 8x11 page, draw this image for yourself, as simply as you can. About two thirds up from the bottom of the page, draw a 1.5" straight line beginning from the outside edge of the page. On the very edge/end of it, add a little stick figure.

Beginning at the opposite edge, across from that little figure, draw another straight line, this one about 3.5". Add some pointed mountains sticking up- far higher that the stick figure is in her horizon.

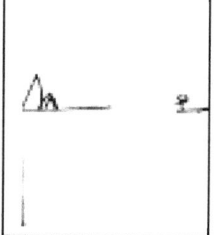

Populate that longer line with whatever comes to mind.
Draw images or write words to articulate what you see there. And there may well be spaces along the line. That is fine too. On the line behind the stick figure draw a small house with a fence around it, with a path leading to this edge.

You will return to this image with the next exercise

(Note To Self...)

JOY THROUGH DISCIPLINE – EMPOWERMENT THROUGH RESPONSIBILITY

To be empowered, very simply you need to find ways by which you can authorize yourself to know your own story, sanction your personal truth, entrust that to those to whom you choose give it, and thus ratify the magic that is yours. Not simple enough? Empowerment is when **you** embrace and own your magic, through the courage, freedom and joy found in the personal story. That magic is the energy/power that we all carry in our Being - the capacity to see, be and do.

That earth-based wisdom, Shamanism, understanding that we are all a part of the power-full forces of nature, recognizes and honors a natural movement toward community through the individual. Magic is not an invisible intangible, but is observable behavior, how you interact with others in your community and in the world.

As I wrote near the end of Chapter 1, when you reach into your Soul, through the Heart and listen to your Spirit's truth, you are indeed magic and powerful. There is no one way to open into that place, and no one can do it for you. Your magic and your power are not handed to you, and do not depend on a guru or priest to manifest. It is solely your creation and your responsibility.

JOY is the feeling you have when you know you are doing what you are meant to do, without thinking about it, analyzing it or often even understanding it. In Shamanic terms, it is when Soul and Spirit are in harmony, when your Power (or Life Force) is moving on your personal Spirit's path.

The world you live in, your upbringing, and the history you carry in your DNA and this current lifetime, generally all serve to disconnect you from that Joy. Therefore, it takes a certain amount of discipline to regain it. In the Introduction I said that you may have to learn to walk before you could fly, that you would have to practice to become the magician you are. And that is where Discipline comes in. You probably have much to unlearn in order to actually get down to/up to/into where your Power lies. And you are not always well supported by your environment and people in your life on your journey back to Joy. But it is Your Journey and Your Joy and so it is hardly surprising that it is also Your Discipline.

I think it is a neat little paradox that the Empowerment that comes with being in Joy entails a certain Responsibility as well. Just as the journey to Joy requires Discipline, so when you have that Empowerment, it will only remain if you behave with Responsibility. It takes Discipline and Responsibility to grow your Empowerment, (and thus open you to your Joy,) and that will stay with you only if you behave Responsibly. A circle, a spiral, but not a straight line to nowhere.

Those are big words no doubt loaded with a lot of your history!

Time to create the next chapter in your book.

_____'s Personal Magic 9

Return to the previous drawing. Add Personal Magic 9 to the 8.

Beginning at the bottom of the page, between the two horizontal lines, draw a spiral up to the level of the lines, in the space between them. Draw at least six turns, each one long enough (they can be as wide as almost 3 inches!) and separated enough to write on the lines between each turn of the spiral.

On the bottom first line write – Responsibility.
On the next – Discipline.
And on the third – Empowerment.

And repeat that for next three turns.

After each word jot down an immediate response to the word, what it means to you. If you need more space, you can spin off the spiral to the bottom and circle back up to the top of the level of the horizons. Write in these turns, though, not straight lines.

(A circle, a spiral, but not a straight line to nowhere.)

Above the gap and horizons, across the middle, draw a large circle. Inside that circle, write a letter to yourself. *Beginning* "Dear *(your name)*
I authorize you to access your magic. You have a right to live as an empowered being. You will know you are

Empowered when you.... *(and fill that in with your own words...)*

Joy will feel .... "

Sign the letter with your name...... and underneath that, "aka...." and the name of your choice - Spirit, God, Creator or whatever language works for you.

Look at your little stick figure. (Yes, it is you as well!) Choose how to get her/him across the chasm. Maybe the spiral has reached to the top and can be walked across. Maybe there is ladder to throw across the gap. Maybe she has a pair of wings in her back pack. Maybe she can walk on air! Be Creative, let your imagination see the solution and say YES!

Finally, spend a little time with the image you have created. Get out the colored pencils and paint, decorate this page further. Take this piece of art, and hang it up somewhere. It is a reminder of your possibilities, and of the combination of tools you have at your disposal.

(Note To Self...)

COUNSELORS, THERAPISTS, GURUS, LIFE GUIDES, SPIRITUAL LEADERS, ETC.

Why do you want one?

Do you need one?

What do you see him/her doing for you? with you?

How to find one, how to trust one, how to evaluate your relationship with one.

How long to spend with one....

(Did you think that I was going to answer those questions?! Not in this book! And anyway, they are your questions - or they should be. So, you need to find the answers!)

As much as this is your Joy and your Discipline, as well as Responsibility and Empowerment, there are times when you will need support, guidance and even a kick in the pants. Knowing how to know when you have the right WHO to help you on a journey is perhaps one of the greatest challenges of any exploration of any kind.

What analogy to use? Perhaps it is like getting a tennis coach? Do you want a parent? a friend? a famous coach who has coached the famous? an ex-tennis player? Or will you get a book or a stack of DVDs and work it out against a wall in the back yard? How long do you need him/her for? Do you outgrow one and find another? When do you know that?

Or is it like going on a 5-day hike? You work out, so you are, well, fit enough (although you will be a bit sore the first day or so, especially if it is mountainous terrain). You get the maps, the right boots, a decent pack, plenty of water, sunscreen and a jacket in case the weather changes. You know what you need because you read books, talked to other hikers and used a certain amount of common sense. (You looked out at the sky, smelled the air and got the 5-day forecast).

In this case it is perhaps a lifelong hike, and as time goes on you will become more proficient and try different paths as well as sticking to the ones you know work for you. Sometimes you will sleep at a hostel and other times under a tree. Sometimes you will hike with another, sometimes entirely alone in nowhere, or you may just stop… And then stumble across those boots again and the map and remember you are on a journey. You might need to get a new pack (the cat has been sleeping in the old one) or work out a bit, but the skills will be there.

Whatever you do, ultimately it is yours to do and let no one tell you otherwise. If you feel your confidence drown in a sea of self-loathing, then you are not on the right path. This doesn't mean the hike won't sometime be steep up or down, wet and cold or burning hot, that you won't sometimes run out of water, walk down a dead end or come face to face with a bear. But you will know when you have been kidnapped or are being shoved off a cliff with no bungee cord. Then get out.

You are the storyteller. It is your story, your magic and your Empowerment. In that relationship between You and the Other, be aware of the Intention of the Interaction. Summarized simply: counselors guide the journey - expect change, are in the lead or at best co-lead; therapists interpret the journey - aim for and expect change and are in the lead; artists participate in the journey - no change expected - and follow the storyteller, sharing the journey and stepping away when their bit is done.

Where do gurus and guides and spiritual leaders fit in? Depends on the guru, guide and spiritual leader. Use your common sense, also called God-given sense and perhaps just intuition, a hunch, a feeling. Pay attention to those! Practice discernment, which is the art of critical thinking, as well as simply paying attention to your intuition. The word 'icki-ness' is useful here. It is not fear, or resistance, but a kind of repulsion and distrust that arises from within you.

As you become more familiar with your Soul and can stay in Awareness of Self, that state of Nonattachment, you will more easily recognize when your ego-self is resisting and when you know that something is not right. The critical thinking part comes when you then ask around about this helper.

Interview them and ask questions of others who have worked with them. This is more important than getting married, buying a house, a car, a college education. In fact it is all that and more. You are going to be in communion with your true Self, you will be building a place from which to live and be, you will venture into the world from there, and you will be forever growing, uncovering wisdom and knowledge from the universe of colleges within.

When you are not desperately wanting rescue, but quietly seeking support with an open mind and heart, you will find the support as/when/if you need it.

PERSONAL MAGIC

Know that no one can save you, no one can hand you the magic wand, and certainly you can't buy it. You have to uncover it. And know that you can.

If you are never asked what you feel, what you know, where your instincts take you, to draw or paint or dance or sing or write a story, then ask why not? And do it anyway.

The Empowered Self is the Magic Self, and the Magic Self is the Empowered Self.

To Recap:

- Empowerment of Self is strengthened and nurtured when you consciously acknowledge and offer your Personal Magic.
- Power is the Life Force of our Soul that activates Spirit.
- Real Power is turned outward to engage the world and not used to pull inward. (That is in the service of the small self, and will diminish you.) The Empowered Self (the Greater Self) grows in Power as s/he engages in the world, however that manifests, which can be very quietly and privately.
- Personal Responsibility and Discipline are required both to access and then to retain empowerment.
- Joy is the felt experience of your Power/Life force (Soul) in harmony with being and doing as your Spirit's path/calling has asked of you.
- This is your magic, your life, and any support systems/individuals are simply that - support. Choose them carefully and be conscious of when the one who is right for you at that time arrives. And when it is time for you to step away on your own again.

_____'s **Personal Magic 10**

Cheat Sheet For Recognizing the Guide You Need

Write responses to these questions.

Do them quickly, one after the other, without thinking too much.

The Other

Who in your life has been your most IN-effective teacher?

Who has been the most Effective?

Make a list of the traits you would want in a guide/teacher.

What do think the role of the guide/teacher is?

You

How do you handle being challenged?

What happens when your comfort zone is rattled?

What most scares you about working closely with another on your personal stuff?

What most comforts you about that?

What is it another can do to inspire or encourage you?

What can they do that defeats or overwhelms you?

How much do you want to learn and evolve?

Close your eyes.

Imagine that the perfect assistant is sitting with you - maybe side by side, maybe across a table.

S/he has all the traits you want and need.

Look into their eyes.

Ask them if they will help you.

Let them ask you if you want their assistance.

Agree to work together.

Lay out some ground rules:

 what you will do - how you will handle the challenge.

 what the guide will do - how he/she will nurture you and hand you the final responsibility.

Pay attention to how this respectful, autonomous collaboration feels.

Imagine how the collaboration will end.

You will no longer need this guide. You will have come into a place of disciplined responsibility. You will know it is time to go and will do so not from fear or anger but from a place of empowerment.

Pay attention to how this feels.

As you leave this guide notice that you are larger, stronger and, in fact, you are your own guide in many ways now.

Go back to the Cheat Sheet and refine it as needs be.

This is simply a touchstone for being aware of your needs and fears as well as being open to the right Guide when (if) they arrive. And also to acknowledge that you probably have most of what you need. You simply may need assistance to access it and develop an attitude of disciplined responsibility.

(Note To Self...)

CHAPTER FOUR

EMPOWERMENT & FREEDOM

THE HERO IN YOUR STORY

Why be empowered at all if it doesn't give you all the material tangibles that you want? *And* is a whole lot of work and responsibility? Because, if nothing else, when you are empowered -that is, fully in Awareness of Selfand knowing from within your Soul -you are quite simply Free. You are free from being at the mercy of others. No one can *make* you anything. No one can make you sad, angry, happy or guilty. You are free to respond as you truly are - not as your ego or your history demands. People can and will still do things that affect you emotionally but what you *do* with that in the form of feeling and behavior is up to you. That is real power, and it is real freedom.

Freedom, according to my little desk dictionaries, can be defined as 'personal or civil liberty,' 'able to do something at will,' 'ease in action,' and 'boldness of conception.' (These last two are precisely what we are able to do when in the creative state!) The other freedoms are only extensions of these basic precepts.

In short, it is being able to choose. It doesn't mean changing what *is* except in how you perceive, understand and then relate to it. It may mean being better able to change it, once you are free from the entanglements of emotional turmoil. It does mean you are less likely to expend energy by trying to make 'things' change when it is not possible, and you will certainly be ready when a new opportunity presents itself.

I think of Empowerment as you being your own hero (or heroine) rather than a victim. Sit with that a moment: how would this change your life? Look back at the image you created for Personal Magic #4. What if you were able to appreciate yourself as the hero in your story, free from being one of the people on the periphery, or the means by which the hero does his/her thing, or worst of all - the slave? Real heroes, not just those of whom we tell battlefield tales, live their lives with courage, honor and in the service of their community.

Much has been written about heroes, heroism and heroic deeds. Most relevant to your journey are the stories of those individuals who, in the face of great odds, and often the derision of others, quietly go about their work and their calling. Certainly no hero is ever a victim, regardless of the circumstances.

In theatre, as actors, our task is to find the journey our character is on, by looking at the given circumstances (the what, where, who and how) and then asking "What is it I (the character) want? What is the goal, the objective of this journey?" By placing the character firmly at the center of the story, the actor is able to inhabit fully the emotional, psychological and behavioral world. The best actors, and the ones with the most courage, also access the spiritual or Soul aspect of their character.

There is an old adage, 'There are no small roles, only small actors.' Likewise, there are no small people, only the small self. By embracing your Personal Magic and bringing that to the world, you can be the hero at the center of your story. You will know your given circumstances, name your goal, and fully inhabit the emotional, psychological and behavioral aspects of your story. Most wonderfully, in real life you can do so without being a puppet at the mercy of some other writer. Rather *you* the writer *and* the director *and* the lead actor.

Bringing these two concepts together, the empowered person is both the hero and the storyteller, is both at the center and also outside the story, able to see it all. The hero doesn't escape the story nor is he/she devoured by it. The real hero/heroine is truly Free and Empowered.

_____'s Personal Magic11

Playwright/Hero

Recall a contained, short scene in your life, with one other person, where you were afraid to speak up and so you didn't. Choose something that did not have a truly awful outcome, but something reasonably safe with which you can practice.

Fill in this Program:

PERSONAL MAGIC

Characters:

        Names

        Ages

        Gender

        Relationship to each other

Location:

        Where the incident took place

        Time of day/night

        Temperature

        Any Distinguishing Feature of the place

The Set Up:

        what happened *right before* this conversation (a few short sentences)

Conflict: (a single brief sentence for each)

        Character A wants...

        Character B wants...

The Dialogue:

VERSION ONE

This is the one where you didn't speak out.

It may be only 6-10 lines of dialogue, and you end up silently going along with the situation/criticism, whatever.

Set it out on the page as dialogue, line by line.

A:

B:

A:

B:

etc

(and remember to name the page Personal Magic 11)

At the end of the dialogue, write a *short* description of what happened next. Write this as if watching a movie with no words, just the visuals and maybe a sound effects or musical sound track. How do you look in relation to the Other in the scene?

Put this story aside.

Look at the drawing that you did in Chapter 1, Personal Magic 4. Breathe into that colorful person at the center of the story.

Look at the drawing you did in Chapter 2, Personal Magic 7. Practice non-attachment.

Look at the art you created in Chapter 3, Personal Magic 9. Embrace your empowerment.

Go back to your basic information - the who/where/what.

The Dialogue:
<u>VERSION TWO</u>
This is the one where you DO speak out.

It maybe only 6-10 lines of dialogue, but you end up naming your need, voicing your disagreement.

Set it out on the page as dialogue, line by line.

A:

B:

A:

B:

etc

(start a new page and name it...)

You will only use words, you will not use physical contact; you will know what to let go of and what to stick to.

At the end of the dialogue, write a *short* description of what happened next. Write this as if watching a movie with no words, just the visuals and maybe a sound effects or musical sound track. How do you look in relation to the Other in the scene?

Maybe you 'won' - changed the other person or the situation - maybe you were simply heard. However it worked out, you stood in your Empowerment.

(Note To Self...)

FREE OF FEAR

Fear has invaded and now drenches our society. Fear of the future (what might happen) and of the past (what we believe happened and therefore - fast-forward into the future - might again....); fear of what we don't have and what we do have; fear of people and places, cultures and religions we don't know or understand. Fear of people we do know. (Can I trust them?) In short, we are fearful of what we know *and* what we don't know. Our social and governmental systems tend to utilize fear as a means by which we are kept 'in control.'

That only works until the fear boils over, and control, self- or societal, vanishes in a rash of many kinds of violence. When we are full of fear, we look to others or to objects for comfort, to calm our fears, to provide answers, to provide meaning. And we panic when that which is outside us does not provide the hoped for security.

The greatest fear, and it weaves through all those above, is the fear of the unknown. What you don't know terrifies you. If your fear is based on a past event it is the fear that it MIGHT happen again that drives you. If you knew for sure you might be able to take action, but you don't know and so you wait for it, not knowing if it will be today or tomorrow or next year.

Underlying all of that fear is fear of yourself. If you don't know who you are how can you know anything else? Achieving Awareness of Self is your beginning out of all that fear. Its greatest gift to you is that it shows you that it doesn't matter that you don't know. With Awareness of Self you can learn to engage ambiguity. You begin live fully and thrive with *not knowing*.

The journey that you are on requires that you be curious without judgment. By all means, *want* to know, be curious, be interested in the story. And if the answer doesn't come at once or at all, if you have to wait and see what occurs, then that IS the story! (Remember in Chapter 2, the first stage of 'self'? that baby, very young child who is curious and accepting of every thing? without judgment? A pretty good basis by which to continue to approach the world and your life.)

Trust your inner wisdom/instincts to know when something is not right, but give it a chance before you rush headlong into fear. In fact, if you are not caught up in judgment -and fear is the worst form of judgment - you *will* know what to do. So often your state of mind interferes with Knowing. And if there is something truly wrong? Something that is actually threatening to your wellbeing? Whether it is physical or psychological (not all attacks are made with a gun) your *response* will be your best defense, rather than a knee-jerk reaction. A *reaction* is just that, an automatic A-leads-to-B behavior that leaves little if any room for Choice. A *response* is choosing what to do in any given circumstance, not from fear and need, but for that place of nonattachment.

You will respond fast enough if you have to, and other times you may take more time. You may choose a very fast response because there is not a lot of time for emotional think. You will be clear and steady, as we so often are in our most immediately challenging experiences. All the 'but what if' anxious self stuff goes out of the window, and your core Being steps in. You do or say exactly the right things that you didn't know you knew how. Or you may move and speak more slowly, taking time to step consciously into your Personal Magic, without the emotional ego directing the show. In either scenario, you will be coming from your center, your Soul, the empowered Self

Empowerment means that you can live without fear. Awareness of Self will help get you in there, and Personal Magic is an expression of living free from fear.

_____'s Personal Magic 12

Think of a place that you have always wanted to go, or an activity you have always wanted to do, but have not done because you were too anxious about how it might *not* work. Take a little time to get a clear image of that place or the activity - where, with whom (or alone.)
Be ready to jot down notes. Take out a new piece of paper and name it, with Personal Magic 12.

Now, go back to that Stage 1) Barely self aware baby (Chapter 2, Personal Magic 5)
Do the first part of the exercise through including listening to your own body sounds, heart-beat, breath and blood moving.
Stop.

Return to the place, activity you have always wanted to go or do. On the piece of paper make a 'Curious About' list. Start by asking and trying to answer questions about the activity or place itself - not about the 'how to', but the 'what is'.

In short, you are now about 2 or 3 years old and full of 'Why/What' and not at all concerned with 'How To'.
Ask things like 'when did this place arrive here' and then all the questions that flow from that.

Ask 'when did people start doing (whatever it is)' and then the questions that flow from that.
Wonder who discovered it, invented it, marketed it, named it. The focus is on the place of activity or place itself, not your role in it.

Next, imagine you can touch, it smell, taste it, hear it, see it. Engage all the senses in the experience.

If there is something you don't know or cannot imagine, allow yourself that it is alright *not* to know.

Now you have arrived at practicing the skill of Engaging Ambiguity. It is perhaps the most nerve-wracking place to be unless you have convinced yourself that you are Not interested in knowing. Then it is easy. However, to be both curious *and* to engage ambiguity? Well, in that there is freedom.

Return to the place that you want to go or activity that you want to do. Put down the 'curious about' list and just sit with the unknown. Remember Chapter 3, Personal Magic 9? The little stick figure who - with responsibility, discipline and empowerment - stepped off the edge of the chasm and safely to the mountains on the horizon? Add Curiosity to your list of tools, and Engaging Ambiguity.

Breathe deeply, releasing any tension in your body. Breathe again, and inhabit that colorful radiant Being who is strong, wise and smart. (Personal Magic 4, Chapter 1) Know now that you can do anything.

Go back to your place or activity and picture yourself there again. Allow that it is a blank canvas, ripe with potential, there for only you to play on. YOU get to fill it in when the time is right.

(Note To Self...)

FEAR OF AGING, DYING AND DEATH

For many, the greatest fears have to do with getting old and dying. The former is shattering to our self image and the latter a step into the absolute unknown. What a *dread-full* combination!

Aging is something that the western culture does not deal with at all well. Everything is set up to avoid it as long as possible. There is make-up, surgery, exercise and diet; there are separate living places (the over 50s, the kids in the other room, etc) so that the generations don't have to spend too much time together. We don't want the young terrified by the old, and we don't want the old envying the young. (Actually, most of the very young love the old, and many of the very old get along just fine with the young.)

Letting go of fear of aging is not to say that you don't take care of your body. When you choose not to participate in the fear around your physical process, you do so not by avoiding age but honoring one of *the triune: body-mind-spirit.* You do so in Awareness of Self - realistically, with curiosity, without judgment and with Joy.

Listen to your body. Observe it and pay attention, with love and respect. Your body is an aspect of your being. It is one of the tools in your kit, a means to an end, not an end. Carry more much weight than your body is meant to, or starve and punish your body by deliberate vomiting, and you are destroying one of the gifts you have been given by which to *be*, to express yourself in the world. Your body is a physical expression of your being in the world and when you live healthily, age gracefully and die peacefully you have truly been a living embodiment of Empowerment and Freedom.

Wonderfully enough with all the advancements in health and wellbeing, 70 is the new 50 and so on. And that gives us an opportunity not to hoard that extension or pretend that we are not repositories of wisdom and skill, but rather to spread it as far as we can!

If we were all eighteen forever, where would we find the grandmothers? For a moment, recall a grandparent, a mentor or older friend. What do they give you? What do you gain from their presence in your life? Honor the old people/elders in your life. You are the beneficiary of their wisdom, experience and the stories they tell.

Honor the old person/elder you are becoming. Offer something that those who come after you will hold in respect and trust.

You don't have to invent a cure for cancer, bake cookies for the neighborhood or write a book. Simply live your life with as much courage, truth and honesty and in your Personal Magic as possible.

_____'s **Personal Magic 13**

(You might feel that you are too young for this exercise. However, if you are older that 10 and not getting younger by the day, it is a valuable activity. If you can get into the habit of celebrating your evolving growth how much easier it will be for you later!)

The Aging Gracefully Booklet
As you embrace growing older consider the ways in which you can honor body, mind and spirit. Remember this is not about refusing the passage of old age, but rather celebrating and honoring it.

Create a little booklet, one of those tiny ones with a note per day. Take a blank 8x11 page, fold it in half, then half again, and now one more fold. When you open it up you should have 8 rectangles. You can cut these into separate pieces, stack them together and staple into a 'book'. Or simply keep them as one folded piece of paper. (When you unfold it you will also 'unfold' the booklet.)

On the left-hand side of <u>each</u> rectangle, as a list evenly spaced beneath each other, write:

Body

Mind

Spirit

After each write one thing that you can do to honor and care for each of the triune.

(For example:

Body - drink more water, photograph my hands, give one of my old coats to someone

Mind - read an article, tell someone a story from my past, make a list of who gets what when I go

Spirit - listen to my heart beating, put my hands in the earth, meditate daily

What honors and nurtures YOUR body, mind and spirit is particular to you. Shut out the cacophony of the anxious, frightened civilization that surrounds most of us. Listen to your Soul and go from there.

(Note To Self...)

HEALING, HEALTH AND MAGIC

There is another advantage if you are not afraid of your body, aging and illness. You will be more empowered to work *with* your physicians and healers. Fear paralyzes and/or diminishes you in ever so many ways. Step into your Empowerment and take responsibility.

In Chapter 1, when writing about Shamanism and health, I reminded you that medicine is moving (back) toward the mind/body and even Spirit connection. Patient Centered Medicine, where the patient – not the practitioner - is at the center of the story is an aspect of that approach. In short, you are invited to be part of the team of healers, to access your Shaman within. More and more hospitals are including the arts and opportunity to practice the arts in the environment, for professional caregivers, families and most of all, for the person at the center of the story - the patient. 'Patient' - it takes patience to heal, drawing on inner wisdom when seeking information, and courage to proceed even when you don't *know.*

Listen with all of your being and you will know what to say, ask and do. You won't have to be told what to do, you will arrive at that plan *with* your physician, nurse practitioner, healer, whomever. You will be an active participant in your healthcare. You will be the hero in your story and not a helpless footnote.

When you manifest your Personal Magic, that tangible expression of who you truly are, then your sense of Self will not be destroyed by the aging body. When you overcome your fear of being less than perfect, when you can sit with pain, loss of mobility, the certainty of death, then LIFE becomes easier and much more pleasant.

There is something that we are often told in efforts to make us feel better about ourselves. 'You are perfect just as you are.' I had always resisted that. I now understand it as *perfect within*, in the moment I am now. It is not comparative, nor an endpoint. This also applies to the physical self, our exterior.

The exterior is an image, a costume, even a symbol of the Self. It is often also a mask. When physical change occurs, and if it is irreversible, when you can no longer hide behind the mask and the costume, then the Self is exposed. The light that shines then, is not that of your dress or your abs, but is the light of your Heart and Spirit. You want to have that shining Self available to share. That Higher Self, the Soul, will shine through and illuminate even the most tired body. You will be beautiful.

More so, that Awareness of Self - nonattachment, comfort with not knowing - will provide a soothing, safe, powerful and beautiful place from which to travel this last length of earth-path on your journey.

Before the next exercise, what is Personal Magic again? Time to revisit that with a short summary.

Personal Magic is the uniqueness that you, and only you, bring into the world. It is the tangible expression of your connection through your Soul to the Great Spirit, Creator, Higher Power, God, whatever language you wish to use, by which we are all connected. It can be directly accessed through the creative endeavor. Personal Magic both encourages and is encouraged by Awareness of Self, leading to true Empowerment and Freedom, most of all, freedom from fear.

_____'s Personal Magic 14

(This is a good one for scribbling in the margin!)

Reflect on somebody you know now or knew in the past who is old, much older than you.

Is this is a person someone you would wish to be like as you age? Why or why not?

(If you can think of no-one you know/knew personally, then refer to historical figures, characters in movies, books etc.)

Who do/did you know who are/were comfortable with their old age?

Focus on that person's attitude to you, to life, to others around them.

Forget their body or if they are in the care of others now, that is not important.

Simply endeavor to see into their Spirit, their shining Soul and Heart.

Would you say that they are/were in their Personal Magic? How do you experience that?

(If you don't know anyone like this, then imagine the old person you want to be, at the end of your life. How do you want others to experience your Personal Magic in their immediate interactions with you?)

Write a letter to that older person, and tell them what the gift of their age and wisdom has meant to you. (Do this on one of the blank pieces of paper. You don't need to send it, although of course you could. It would brighten their day!)

(Note To Self...)

THE POWER OF GIVING

Empowerment is a responsibility, requires constant attention and often leads to ongoing commitments to others as well as ourselves. So, apart from Freedom, why are we driven to pursue it? I think that it arises out of the innate human desire – perhaps even need - to Give. (I am speaking of those things that bring 'good' not harm. When giving brings harm it is not in order to assist another; it is rather to get something for yourself. Then it is not a gift but a form of coercion.)
In Chapter 3 I told you that power is only power when it turns itself outward, in the service of others, rather than serving a narrow little self or ego. We are in our greatest power when we give.

Try the following exercise. Do it quickly - jot notes rather than writing an essay! Write directly onto this page. It *is* your book after all.
(And you have that wide margin there.)

Remember a time when you *took something* that was not yours.

Where were you?

How old?

What was the 'thing'?

How did you get it?

How did the other person look/behave to you afterwards?

What did you do with it?

How do you feel now….

Now remember a time when something that had meaning was *given to you*.

Where were you?

How old?

What was the 'thing'?

How did you get it?

How did the other person look/behave to you in the giving?

What did you do with it?

How do you feel….

And finally remember a time when you *willingly gave* something (good) to another.

Where were you?

How old?

What was the 'thing'?

How did you give it?

How did the other person look/behave to you at that moment?

What did they do with it?

How do you feel now….

When you are empowered, you can choose what to receive (allow in) and what to give (offer out). The feelings - and indeed the tangible outcome of giving - often elicit a smile on the face of the giver as well as the receiver, a sensation of warmth, peace of mind. Most of us want to feel good, to be at peace. Giving a welcome gift with an open heart and with no expectation of 'reward' brings its own reward - of goodness, of peace and of honorable power.

Perhaps counter-intuitively, you are most empowered when you give, and the gifts that have the greatest capacity to stimulate empowerment are those that are created with courage and truth, offered as gifts with no expectation of reciprocity. A gift is only a gift if offered as such. When we place a condition or price on it, it becomes a 'deal' or a sale.

Think back to the odd art objects a child made for you, the original hand-written love poem, or the songs you and your friends made up and 'performed' in the car together, and you will remember what I mean.

(An aside: while I believe that the best gifts are those you have made yourself, to select a gift from another artist with perfect attention and empathy toward the person to whom you will give it, can be as powerful. However, do take the time to wrap it, create a personal note, and give it away as the artist *you* are.)

What *is* a gift? I turned to those desk dictionaries for a brief look and found this: 'natural endowment, talent, faculty miraculously bestowed' (*Oxford English Dictionary*). And this: 'the act or power of giving' (*Random House*). '*Miraculously bestowed....power of giving.*' Well!

So how was it that 'Power' became something that turned inward, that lost its connection to giving? I think it has to do with that fear.... When you are afraid of losing, when you see nothing but 'not enough,' and live without connection with your own Soul, then you reach out and grab for all that you can out of fear. You forget how to give, because you are so afraid of the unknown, the future. So you grasp at the past, and try and to fortify yourself against the future. Practice giving. It might just save you by revealing your Self/Soul to you!

What if the gift is not appreciated or is ignored? If you have created it from your personal place, creating your own magic, then it still has value. The value is in the act of creation. Oddly, when you are at your most 'selfish' (that is, interested in Self/Spirit, in seeing your truth, when you are aware and courageous) then you are also at your most generous. The act of creation is first and foremost a gift to and of yourself, and then you give away the 'object' or thought or love. (Note: this is different from giving yourself away. You are the goose that lays the golden egg - keep yourself and give away the eggs!)

The corollary to giving is the capacity to receive. In Awareness of Self, you will know when a gift is being given freely and you will be able to accept it freely. You will have the empowerment to recognize and honor a gift being offered you. This means without guilt or toting up the value, what you owe in return. Equally, if you know how to give and receive a gift (and here is the real magic), you will also have the empowerment to say 'no' to that which you don't want to let in. You will recognize that which harms and you will have the strength and courage to decline it. As well, you will probably be able to do it in a manner that does not harm the other. Now that IS magic!

Gift giving and receiving is really only possible with individual empowerment, and that can, and often does, extend out into community. (I will address that more in Chapter 6.) You might ask, "How can the 3 year old who decorates the paper plate and gives it to me be empowered?" Surely they are too young to have done the work.' Perhaps though, it is because s/he *is* so young and has not become enmeshed in the coils of self-consciousness, that the giving is so spontaneous, open and honest.

To Recap:

- The Empowered Hero/Heroine lives in Freedom, both creator and star in the story of his/her life.
- Fear - of the unknown, of yourself - is what keeps us small and powerless. Awareness of Self and your Personal Magic is a way to pass through that.
- Add Curiosity and Engaging Ambiguity to your Personal Empowerment tool kit
- You will learn to live comfortably without knowing the answers to everything because you will know *your* Spirit.

- Practice Nonattachment, trust your intuitions and instincts without too much Thinking, and you will respond as fast or as carefully as the story requires.

- Fear of Aging and Death is a product of fear of the unknown and disconnect from your Soul/Life Force with its power to access Spirit.

- Respect and honor your physical self without fearing its changes.

- Honor your wisdom - wherever it is found

- Be your own Healer, working as a responsible, empowered individual in collaboration with your other healers and physicians.

- The Power of Giving - and Receiving. By fully immersing yourself in your Personal Magic, you will have the most to give, thus enhancing your empowerment. When you are Empowered you can receive gifts freely and you can recognize and decline that which you do not want - or need - in your life.

_____'s Personal Magic 15

(you may need to take a trip to the store before you can do this!)

Get out your colored pencils, crayons and/or paints. Use blank paper, preferably larger heavier paper than the regular 8x11s, although that will work as well. Sketching paper would be great! Have on hand scissors, glue, maybe a stapler, colored construction paper, stickers, old magazines. Take some time to gather these things and then come back to the Gift Giving. (If you don't have elementary school age kids in the house, you can always raid the Dollar Store or Michaels if they are having a sale.)

Now, here you are back and you have a pretty good beginning on an Arts Tool Kit – a gift to yourself!
Put in the CD (you have that right?)
You have the length of time it takes for the CD to play to complete the gift.

Now, with the music playing, simply allow yourself to draw, color, cut and glue.
As you are creating this work of art, begin to picture *to whom* you might give it. Someone you trust, someone who will value the gift. It might be someone you know or someone at a shelter, in a hospital, or an assisted living center. You will come to know as you are creating the art. (Engaging Ambiguity!)

Let the art tell you where (if not actually to whom) and allow that awareness to shape the art. You may find that you add words, or specific mages, it may be simply random shapes and colors.

As the piece is taking shape decide *when* you will give it.
Ideally it will in the next day or so and you can do it in person.
If not, mail it to someone the very next day.

When the CD finishes, put everything away - everything.
The gift is made. You have been in a deep place of creation, from your Soul. It cannot be improved from here. It must leave your possession. Don't take photos or put it on Facebook.

Simply give it to someone you know will value it. This is important. Choose carefully. It is about the person who receives the gift.

After you have given this gift, come back to the exercise and describe the actual moment of giving. The look in other's face, how they explored the gift, and *then* how you felt.

*** This is a really important step in this exercise. Write on a piece of paper and name it Personal Magic 15.

If they seemed surprised, were quiet, puzzled or even maybe dismissive, know that it could be because not many people are used to receiving gifts without strings. Some are wary. HOW YOU give is the key.

When you practice giving with no expectation of return, when you learn how to give and to whom, then it will become easier and easier. The value of the gift will not diminish but you, the gift giver, will be more at ease with it and less attached to the outcome.

If you find this way too daunting, then bake something, sew or replant something. Even carefully considering what and where to purchase a gift, solely for the enjoyment of another person, calls upon your expression of creativity. The intention of giving is to bring your creativity to the choice of gift and to so without expectation of return.

(Note To Self...)

PERSONAL MAGIC

CHAPTER FIVE

STEPPING INTO YOUR PERSONAL MAGIC

By now you know the touchstones of
Personal Magic (spirit, creativity,
awareness of self) and the aspects that
go into manifesting that Magic
Empowerment and Responsibility), and

you know why empowerment is worth all the effort. When
you are in your Personal Magic you are free.
In this chapter you are heading into the *How To* bit.

You will notice there is a certain circularity in this: 'Access
your Personal

Magic to be Empowered - Empowerment allows the
expression of your

Personal Magic.'

That is because they are really the same thing. One is the
inner experience (Empowerment) that is expressed on the
outside (Personal Magic) and yet the outside expression is
essential to sustain the inner. We are, after all, beings that
are inherently connected to all within our environment, to
the earth, sky, water and air, and all the expressions of form
thus created. Your individual Personal Magic contributes to
that greater whole, and the Power of that greater whole in
turn sustains and empowers each individual whom makes up
that whole.

When you withdraw your connection from the whole, when you shrink from bringing your Personal Magic into the environment, then you are starving yourself and limiting your wellbeing and potential in proportion to the amount you actively withhold. Remarkably though, you don't have to give a lot or give big or even give materially in order to be an equal shareholder in the Universe. You have simply to give; your truth, your love, your awareness. Remember, your Personal Magic is just that, magic that is both yours and unique to you. Its tangible expression is your living of it, and if along the way an 'object' is created, so be it. You will know what your Personal Magic is and how that is manifest when you step into it.

In Chapter 3 I wrote:

'... *to be empowered, very simply you need to find ways by which you can authorize yourself to know your own story, sanction your personal truth, entrust that to those to whom you choose give it, and thus ratify the magic that is yours. Not simple enough? Empowerment is when* **you** *embrace and own your magic, through the courage, freedom and joy found in the personal story.'*

Simply: To authorize (own) and to sanction (permit) is to *give voice to*; to entrust (give) and to ratify (confirm) is to *put out into the world* that which is truly yours.' How to do that?

LETTING GO

A key step is to let go of anything and all that keeps you stuck in your small self. When you hold on to those things that keep you contained and small then you cannot really tell and live your own story in the world. (Remember in Chapter 4, I told you about being the hero in your story? Be the writer, director and lead actor or character.)

I think that when we talk about letting go it is much easier said than actually done. You can say 'I am letting go,' breathe deeply in and out, and tell yourself you are no longer angry, sad, resentful, disappointed or wanting something. However, that can be like pulling a blind down on a room, a blanket over your head, having an extra drink to blot out an intensity of feeling. It is merely *covered*, not let go.

And things grow even in the dark….mold, black spiders, cockroaches, infection.

And all these things eventually come back out. You can be surprised, can think it is a new thing to let go of, and the process starts again. But it may not be new, because you didn't really let go. You stuffed away, and that was a neat way to avoid dealing with it. It was not let go - it was self righteously (and often with a sickly-sweet air of martyrdom or dramatic magnanimous gesture) shoved under the waters of awareness.

Letting go is painful, self-revealing, difficult and, I believe, an ever-ongoing process. Lift up the stone under which you stowed the 'letting go,' with intention and as a choice, not just when you stub your toe on it. Look under and ask if what you see growing there is the old stuff. However, if, when you lift the stone, the earth is clean, damp, smooth, and the bottom of that stone is free of clinging webs and spores, then indeed you have let go.

Metaphor is all very well, but what do I mean in actual, practical terms? I see three steps.

First, letting go means truly seeing your own part in the event, the interaction, relationship. It means owning your fears, wants, and hurts. It means looking truthfully at 'what if I keep this?' and 'what if I let it go?' Answer each of those with a list of pros and cons. This entails really asking yourself and answering 'what do I get from holding on?' and also 'when I let it go, what do I lose?' Acknowledge feelings of embarrassment, inadequacy, judgment, power-over. It is not easy to do!

And then secondly, it means forgiving - really forgiving, not in expectation of being forgiven in return but in terms of forgiving *the other AND yourself.*

Letting go applies to dreams, hopes, anything that to some degree depended on others doing their part in your 'play.' These have to be truly let go. Throw that script away... and don't continue to wish that it had been. Admit you are helpless to change the past and have no real way of forcing the future in any real sense (although you may be able to temporarily blackmail an individual into a certain behavior, yourself included.) Accept that you only have yourself and the present in which to be fully engaged.

And thirdly, what if you can't let go? Then don't pretend that you have. It does no one any good. You fool yourself, harbor resentment and guilt, and are in continual disappointment. To return to the metaphor, the dark place under the rock hatches a host of attached grievances, and the original issue builds in power. Acknowledge that the gains of holding on to the dream, grievance, whatever, are currently greater than those of letting go. Allow yourself a return to step one if indeed it still seems to be something that you want to release. Dig a little deeper, find the root in your own story and try again.

(You might find you are doodling like mad here in the margin!)

By now you may have thought, 'Mmm, this is a bit like nonattachment.' Yes it is. And so letting go and nonattachment are the twin sisters on the way to Awareness of Self. Or are they the children of Awareness of Self? This is not necessarily a 'do this first and then this' process, but a spiral on which we walk, returning to skills and tools as we build the next layer, and from that layer back to the skills and tools.

Letting go is not for the fainthearted, the lazy or the one-shot wonders. It requires you to grow and keep on growing, It offers endless opportunities for Awareness of Self and developing new skills, as well as to hone old ones. Letting go is not vaporizing something. It is more exposing it to the light and to fresh air, so that it is purified and transformed into something translucent. Ultimately, it is something that has been disassembled altogether.

It is possible, it is desirable and it is for each individual to bring about on his or her own, irrespective of any other person's stories, past or present. Letting go is a personal private matter with a ripple effect that can only be a byproduct and not a goal. Free yourself and then others will be free.

_____'s Personal Magic 16

LETTING GO

Think of something you do really want to let go of. It is perhaps at this stage best not select the biggest one in your life but substantial enough to use as practice.

Sit comfortably in your chair, feet on the floor.

Take a couple of deep breaths, release them slowly and completely.

With each release get a clearer memory of the event/interaction that led to the hurt, anger, embarrassment that you want to let go.

Do the following on a piece of paper, named with your name and Personal Magic 16.

Using this scene, write out as the Script Program (Chapter 4, Personal Magic 11) with Characters, Location, The Set Up and the basic Conflict.

Now, bisect the page into two columns on the page

Name one 'If I let this go what happens?'

Name the other 'If I keep this what happens?'

Now, really answer those questions - there may be pros and cons to each.

Thus you may have 'If I let this anger go then I will feel sad.'

and at the same time 'If I let this anger go then I won't feel anxious every time I see her'.

You might have, 'If I keep this relationship then at least I will have someone to go out with.' *and* 'If I let it go then I won't have to put up with his drinking.'

Be honest with yourself.

Now go over the list and rate each on a scale of 1-3 (3 = Very important , 1 = not very.)

Now, if you still want to let it go, take the next step.

Revisit Chapter 2, Personal Magic 7. In the rectangle (movie screen) write the above scenario.

On each little audience head write your response to it. Connect those little heads to the Ocean (your soul) and then to the sun/spirit. Extend then the suns rays over the entire drawing.

Now, from that place of non-attachment, forgive the other person and forgive yourself. The other for their part in the loop, and yourself for yours. Know that what you wanted and what happened are in the past, and you can't do anything about that.

Know that you cannot control the future either - not the other persons' response to you or whether the universe provides the perfect job or your body type changes.

You do have Now and you have YOU and that is where you need to operate from.

When you have done this, stop thinking about it. Stand up and walk about a bit. Have a glass of water, go outside for a minute.

Come back and look at the Script again.

What do you feel?

If you are still attached, feel the emotional charge of the hurt, fear, anger still kick, then give it more time.

Resist the impulse to say it went away when it is still there.

It is better that you know there may be a deeper level of attachment, of reward and need for this story, or a deeper level of understanding to be reached.

Come back to it another time, write the scene again and pay attention to your part in the story as well as the Other's.

(Note To Self...)

POSITIVE BEING

Another way into your Personal Magic is how you view the world, and your interactions with it. There is a well-used phrase that floats about today - 'positive thinking.' It is a handy hook, a feel-good, hippie-dippie, psycho-pop term. "Oh, think positively." "When things are bad, I use positive thinking." The problem with positive thinking is just that - it is *thinking*. Thinking is a pretty surface-level activity and often doesn't reach deeply enough (or is it high enough?) into our wise Self.

I think real positive thinking is truly seeing what *is*, with clear vision, from an emotionally nonattached place. This requires courage and an *open mind.* And what is an open mind? It is being open to anything, working with what *is*, regardless of what you fear or want it to be.

Positive means being in tune with the universe, aware of and open to something that is greater than the ego, inviting in the Spirit and then truly listening to it. It is not a fighting, demanding or fearful energy. That takes from you, is a negative.

Conversely it is not negative to recognize and engage with the events, circumstances and feelings that may 'feel negative'. In the experiences of loss, fear, sadness and challenge we actually have enormous opportunity to grow. Thus, these are ultimately a vital aspect to Positive Being – in that you are willing and able to recognize this in your life.

Think water not rock.
Think open eyes not blinders.
Think letting go not holding on.

Positive dwells in the midst of actual real life and is not skewed off to the side.
Positive is letting Spirit guide you, opening to the bigger picture and bringing Power/Life Force to your heart and mind.

It is not willing something into being because you are afraid or angry or desperate. That kind of energy is stifling, drowning and heavy.

Being in a positive state often means experiencing some discomfort. It is not simple or simplistic but does require a lightness of touch, a joy and a delight and love. It is a way of being in the world, that accesses something greater than just how you are treated, what you have lost or are working on getting.

Positive Thinking comes from the human ego with its issues of control. (Perhaps it is a close relative of Self-Awareness.) Positive *Being* allows the body-mind-spirit connection to lead the way. This is certainly easier when you come from Awareness of Self . You can see the entire spectrum of what is before you and make choices from there. You do not have to force the facts to fit a picture that will 'make you feel better.' ("When you are free, no one can *make* you anything." Chapter 4.) The facts are just that – facts - and what you do with them is the important part.

It is not how we think *about* life but how we ARE *in* life that makes the difference.

Positive Being requires more of you, right to your roots. It is not a little saying to trot out, it is a deeply felt fundamental way you live. It does not run away from life, it does not presume to dictate. Positive Being demands that you be truthful to yourself and others, release ego-ic attachments, and remain grounded. It is open to *all* possibilities.

So, I prefer Positive Being to Positive Thinking.

_____'s Personal Magic 17

This will require its own page - Personal Magic 17.

Select something about which you tell your self 'Think Positive.'

Now, *be* positive with all the information there is about that event, physical position, whatever, without emotional attachment to outcome.

Jot down the information in any kind of form on the page.

Consider *all* the possible outcomes, different points of view, and allow them to be what they are - *possible, different.*

Make a list of actions you can/will truly take, now.

Make another list of what you cannot change or do right now.

Then sit with what *is*. See the truth without the emotional baggage. See the present state and accept that picture without undue hope, criticism or fear or anxiety. It just *is*.

(If you start to feel anxious, take a minute or two and breathe, consciously in and out. Feel the air move from the top of your head, down through the center of your being to the bottoms of your feet and out to the earth. You will feel grounded and clear.)

Now that is Positive Being. Nothing is hidden, and nothing is pulling at you, and nothing is there that can make you feel inadequate.

(Note To Self...)

When you can let go and live in Positive Being, then you are connected to Spirit.

MEDITATION

Throughout time, it has been known that one key to connecting to your Spirit is through meditation. In the meditative state, you are unmoved by the physical world around you, guided by intuition in the moment, neither seeking to understand the past or foretell the future, nor criticizing the creation as it unfolds.

It is a tool to take you into that place where you can truly be with what is, can 'see' without expectation, 'understand' without judgment and 'know' what you can't think. There has been more written about this, and there are more teachers, books and classes than I can possibly begin to address. Very simply, meditation is a breathing based activity that will help you to stop your mind from thinking, carry you deeply into your higher consciousness and open up your inner know-ing.

It is a form of Awareness of Self and as such takes practice (your self-awareness is very uncomfortable with meditation!) and personal responsibility (no one can meditate for you!).

In my exploration of this form, I have come to this conclusion: it is very easy to get caught up in the RIGHT way to do it and then ego is involved, and judgment and critical faculty are constantly at the table. However, it is worth the effort and the discipline. Along the way you will be uncovering other tools and other awarenesses. They go hand in hand. This Personal Magic journey is like a parade. More and more characters will join you and play in your band, taking it in turns with a solo. However, you hold the conductor's baton. Don't forget that. And together you will create a full rich sound. (Remember the image of Spirit in Chapter 1? Just as you are a member of the universal orchestra, so *you* are the sum of many sounds and melodies.)

As with seeking any support, guidance or encouragement (see Chapter 3), try several different forms, don't give up, and be kind to yourself as you learn where that muscle is and how to use it!

I am not going to so much teach you a meditation technique as share a grounding-clearing-empowering exercise that I do, that can also be called a meditation. I learned this from the Shaman I studied with in Sedona, Arizona, and share it with his permission. (To hear Jade Wah'oo guide you, go to his website http://www.shamanic.net for a free audio.) The written version below is how I practice this particular exercise. If nothing else, it is a wonderful way to breathe, be in the present, and connect with your inner self however that feels for you.

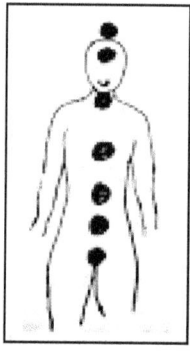

First, a note on language: Chakras are 7 power centers located in a vertical line from below the naval up to the top of the head. (These are also called the 7 Maidens in the Shamanic paradigm.)

Eagles Egg Meditation

Throughout the meditation, do the following:
sit in a chair, feet flat on the floor, hands together at crotch, tips of pointer fingers together, tips of thumbs together, the other fingers interlaced. Breathe deeply and steadily in through your nose and out through your mouth. Allow that your imagination and capacity to visualize images are part of this activity.

Take a few deep, clearing breaths.

Imagine that there is a fluted tubular column, running the length of your spine and on downward connecting you into the ground (Mother Earth).

Picture under each foot a pool of clear clean crystalline water (so, 2 pools) about 18 inches below each foot.

As you breathe in, draw that water up into your feet. As you breathe out, let it ebb back into the ground. Next, breathe in the water up to your ankles and back out. Work your way up your legs and hips in this way. Use the movement of the water to scrub clean any murkiness or pain or discomfort as it flows up and ebbs back.

As the crystalline liquid reaches your belly, and on upward, picture, one at a time, the position of each of the chakras. You may also begin to 'notice' murkiness or discoloration within each. You don't need to intellectualize on what that is; simply let the movement of the liquid cleanse the area.

Remember to keep breathing in through your nose and out through your mouth.

Keep your hands in place while you wash through your body with the liquid. (This doesn't have to take long - you don't have to analyze anything!)

Now picture a golden light above your head (Father Sun). Let this light enter through the top of your head and mix with the crystalline liquid. Together they move through your body and empower you from the inside out. (The ratio liquid to light is as follows; Men: 1/3 liquid, 2/3 light. Women: 2/3 liquid, 1/3 light.) Truly feel the power of this mix flowing throughout your body, all the way to your toes, fingertips, each hair follicle. (*I usually take the time to see it in each chakra one by one, and make sure the color is clear and bright. If it isn't I take a little extra time with it.*)

Now focus on your interlaced fingers and that shape that is created between the pointer fingers and thumb. It is the perfect place to hold an egg. (Keep breathing.) Let that mix flow to your hands and feel/see an egg filled with the light/liquid mix. When the egg is formed and present, through a mental image pull that egg up to the top of your head.

Return your attention to your hands again. Another egg will form; draw that to the top of your head. The first egg will drop down to the next chakra/maiden position (the 3rd eye – in the middle of your forehead).

Focus back on your hands again, and draw the third egg to the top. Each of the previous two eggs will drop down, so now you have a golden egg at the 5th position (throat), the 6th (forehead), and 7th (just above your head).

Continue this process until each of the 7 chakras/maidens are a shining power-center. *(I like to use the breathe-out to draw the mix to my hands and form the egg, and the breathe-in to move it up to the top of my head….the rhythm works well for me.)*Put your attention/mental image on the heart charka. Using your breathing, draw more of the liquid/light mix into that center so that it expands, until it has grown outward to surround you. (It grows by filling with liquid.) You will expand the heart egg until you are inside the egg that is an arm's length above, below, and to each side of you.

You are still connected to Mother Earth through the fluted column.

As you look around the Egg, notice if there are any weak spots or cracks and gently smooth them over with an extra layer of the golden crystalline mix.

Rest a moment.

To complete this meditation: breathe all the way out, bend over so your head is hanging, shake out your hands, and sit up with open eyes.

Context

This egg is not a shield, there to protect, but is a kind of neutral zone, allowing the arrows shot toward you to pass through without sticking. You are not disengaged from the world. You are able to be fully present in the world without expending energy on deflecting or engaging in emotional entanglement. In short, you are in Nonattachment.

Be aware of how this place feels, and know that you can place yourself there any time you need to. If you practice this often enough, the experience of being there is readily accessible to you when you need it suddenly! (Such as the kind of immediate response to threat/attack mentioned in Chapter 4, and more often when you don't have a life-threatening situation but are taken unaware by someone's words or action. You can slip into the Egg and respond from a calm and clear center.)

If you don't 'feel' anything, or 'see' anything, that is okay.

Let your imagination tell the story. This is metaphorical and not literal. The imagery and pattern are helpful for the mind to have something recognizable in order to enter into a meditative state.

If you miss a step, or have to go back, that is fine too. Over time, it will become easy to remember and to do.

The Chakras/ 7 Maidens/Star Sisters' Attributes/Colors
A useful intellectual base that forms a background and set of touchstones for this exercise.

#7 - Purple	crown	awareness of self/ expression spiritual self
#6 - Indigo	3rd eye	intuition, intellect, pattern recognition
#5 - Blue	throat	communication, expression, creativity
#4 - Green	heart	love, compassion, empathy, affinity w/ living things
#3 - Yellow	solar plexus	responsibility, ethics, integrity, power - right use of power
#2 - Citrine	belly	sexuality/mentality
#1 – Red	root/base	physical health and vitality/survival

(You might not see colors, you may hear tones, or have a direct experience.)

_____'s Personal Magic 18

Go back to Personal Magic 17 (Letting Go). Do that again after sitting in this meditation. If you wish to work with a different script that is fine!

(Note To Self...)

THE ARTS AS A WAY TO EMPOWERMENT

Throughout time, it has been known that one key to connecting to your Spirit is Creativity. In the creative state, you are unmoved by the physical world around you, guided by intuition in the moment, neither seeking the future, nor criticizing the creation as it unfolds.

(And if you think you just read most of the above paragraph, well you have, right under Meditation.) We use the word 'magic' to describe something inexplicable that happens, when we are happy, full of wonder, joyful. "It was magical." There has been a transformation of experience out of the day-to-day reality. Magic happens when you relax into the moment of discovery. It is simply being in the awareness of Now. You are operating at a spiritual level. A creative experience can be magical and, like the practice of Shamanic meditation, takes us with intention into that alternate world.

PERSONAL MAGIC

Magic is not so much about *changing what is* as it is about adjusting how you perceive, understand and experience life. (Yes, like Positive Being.) The brainwave patterns associated with both creative and meditative states are similar. And in those states, you achieve distance from the emotional impact of life because you are experiencing your story in the present, the Now. Thus you are interested and curious but nonattached.

Without the interference of the ego, or self-consciousness, you will also *know* more clearly and therefore be able to respond more effectively to what is happening. That 'what' may be creating art after the event to tell your story rather than being trapped within the memory of the story. Through that lens you can understand the events of the story without emotional distress.

By spending time in the meditative or creative state and practicing nonattachment and evolving Awareness of Self, gradually you will be living more and more in that magical state of Empowerment and Freedom. You will rarely be caught unaware. When you are, it will be a quick shift into the place from which you can respond without ego-ic entanglement.

There are so many ways to empowerment: prayer, groups, exercise, family, education, reading great stories, attending inspirational talks, workshops by experts, those endless 'how to' books. The most direct and deep level of empowerment, however, comes from within. Tell your story for yourself and then share it.

The activities/Personal Magic moments in this book (and

particularly this chapter) provide ways in which the arts, and specifically writing, open you to that power. Too often you are enmeshed in the intellect - thinking, problem solving, planning, fixing the past. The arts simply say, "It is this now." As an artist you move beyond understanding (philosophy) and illness/hurt (healing) and become a gift-giver. The journey may (and probably will) involve the other aspects, but in the end you are the creator of your life.

The act of creation transmutes fear and helplessness into courage and power. Magic indeed. YOU are the alchemist, and no matter how many assist you on the way, the ultimate magic arises in and from you.

We all want to be able to create our life, know who we are, change the 'bad' and have more of the 'good.' We wish to be healthy, balanced, wise and kind. We aspire to do good and struggle to find peace within. Begin by telling your story through the arts - writing, visual art, dance and music.

When you give yourself time and place, perhaps with guidance from one who has been there, you will find your truth. Articulate that truth and then, most empowering of all, offer it to the world, however that is defined for you. You are the primary artist in your life, you can make a gift of that life. First you need to uncover/discover your Spirit's path (or Personal Magic), then articulate and send that truth out, as all artists do with their gifts.

It is probably necessary for me to write this right now. Resist the temptation to wait until you have all this down before you start doing it. You can be creating the art as you uncover the path and the converse as well. In fact by doing it you will create and uncover it. If you wait until it is 'perfect' you will miss so much, as will the world, and you will probably never actually find or share it. There is a wise song/poem by Leonard Cohen ('Anthem') with the lines:

> *Ring the bells that still can ring.*
> *Forget your perfect offering.*
> *There is a crack in everything.*
> *That's how the light gets in.*

Let the light in on your story.

The only challenge is not whether you are a writer, a painter, a dancer, or a musician, but whether you have the courage and willingness to really tell/live the story from and of the heart/soul, not the one your intellect wishes to hear. We all have a heart, we all have a soul, we all have a story, and thus we are capable of artistically creating and sharing it.

So what stops you from the creative endeavor? Years of being told your 'art' is not good enough, or that others know you better than you do. ("Oh you don't think that." "Don't be silly." "That's just your imagination." "It's not that big a deal.") Indeed those may be so, but you can only know that for yourself through your personal journey. And it is actually nobody else's business anyway.

Years of turning to experts has meant we have become mired in a kind of imaginal and personal laziness, giving up power to others. We look to parents, teachers, government and specialists to make the rules so that we do not have to take any responsibility at all for whatever happens. (Remember when McDonald's had to put a warning on cups of coffee to tell us it was hot in case somebody spilled it and then sued?)

The guidelines offered by all of the above may well be useful and instructional. Ultimately they are there to offer you information from which to make choices, not to trap you in static helplessness. However, you have to take responsibility for your own story.

What else stops you? Fear - fear of being wrong, looking stupid, being surprised, disappointed, or worst of all, hurt. Perhaps also it is a fear of being free and finding yourself flying. When you are flying, not buried in the mud, hidden in a cave or clinging to a rock in the crashing surf, then what? You are, in short, Empowered - to follow your personal and unique path, create your life, your story. That is Big!

To get there, to get back to that place of Empowerment (because you began there once) begin with telling your story as it has been thus far. Who am I? How am I? My feelings, thoughts, fears, dreams. You will think you know, your mind will jump right in and begin, "Once upon a time... " and then, very quickly it will go on with " and then he did to me" and "she said to me" and "they made me." Or, "I won," "I had to," "I should have," "I failed."

That is not the story of You.

Take a breath, steady yourself, and let the creative spirit, in whatever form and through whatever path, open up the real story. Sometimes it is best not to use many words or narrative. (A to B to C to D etc). Go for plot, that is, move back and forward in time, leave bits out, suddenly add them in elsewhere, jump from image to image, make list of phrases, of words. Maybe there are passages of tangible material description, maybe there is art or a collage, maybe there is a musical interlude. Go for the metaphors, similes, allegory and poetry.

This kind of from-the-heart/soul/gut storytelling will reveal the truth more clearly than any amount of mental gymnastics and careful A to B to C journal-keeping will do. When you free yourself to trust the moments, you will remember and know and see your Soul story. It is this story that will empower you.

So to Recap

- Personal Magic is the Outer expression of Empowerment, the Inner experience. It keeps you connected and empowered.
- Letting Go - truthfully, in a state of nonattachment and with patience. Put away those things that have only negative impact on you. It may take time, but see your part in the story, forgive, and do it properly.

- Positive Being - be fully conscious/aware of all that actually *is*, without attachment to outcome or fixing anything. Be open to all possibilities and come to it in Awareness of Self, and your connection to Spirit.

- Meditation takes discipline and responsibility, and only you can do it. It will open you to new Awareness and is worth the effort to find what works for you and to do it.

- Magic is not illusion but opening your understanding and *knowing*, adjusting perspective from the soul.

- Access the arts to help you arrive at and then express this place - your Personal Magic.

- The cracks let the light in - don't wait until it is perfect. Every one of us is an artist, every one of us has a story, and every one of us can tell it and choose the audience with whom we share it.

- Tell your story now. Be creative and instinctive in the way you do it! It is not a journal but a collage of ever-evolving self, with surprises and joys.

_____'s Personal Magic 19

The following exercise is a combination of two Performing Wellness™ exercises, and will require several pages of paper. Be sure to name the sheaf with your name and Personal Magic 19.

Jumping Off!

Do these Jump Off phrases one at a time.

New page, next prompt; then the next.

• Jumping off the cliff…..

PERSONAL MAGIC

• Sometimes when I dream….

• The view from the top of the mountain….

For each, set a timer for 5 minutes, write the phrase word-perfectly and then keep writing from there. Write without stopping to read what you have written or think about what you might write. Just let the words pour, without regard to spelling, grammar, full sentences or change of direction.

When the timer goes off, stop writing wherever you are, don't read it. Shake out your hands, and then get a new page to write on.

Do the next the same way and time.

Repeat for the third.

You now have 3 pieces of writing.

Now, in the mode of Wild Child - excited, happy, confident (leave the editor and the critic in the closet!) - read each of them one by one.

As you read each, circle 4 words and 4 phrases that Jump Out at you.

Do this fast, don't think about it. They may be jumping out because you can't read it! That is okay. Think of it as beach combing, finding treasures on the sand.

On a Separate piece of paper write each of those circled words and phrases in a column/list - so you will end up with 12 words and 12 phrases in a list, one under the other.

Put aside this first lot of writing.

Using just the circled words/phrases arrange them in any way that comes to The Wild Child. In short - fast, by feel and impulse not by thought and planning.
You may add joining words, you may alter tenses so they match if you want to, however try not to add new words and do include *all* words.

Set a limit of about 10 minutes for this… (use the timer so you don't have to be looking at the clock.)
It may end up looking like a poem or be prose - it doesn't matter.

Write the entire piece out cleanly - leave a space at the top. No Title.
Take a breath - rest.
Now, as if you have never seen this before, the final find on the beach, and with an open heart and curiosity (!) read your new piece right through. When you have done that, there is the title - as soon as you finish reading it The Wild Child will know what it is called. Write that at the top.

You may want to take this piece of art further, by adding visuals and sound to it.
Color the writing and maybe the color changes throughout the piece.
Add what kind of music you might hear with each paragraph, line, word.

This collage of words, color and sound, this unplanned collection of images, feelings and thoughts will be one of the most powerful ways that you come to know your Self.

Trust that this sort of connection through creativity to Spirit will lead you into your Empowerment and Personal Magic.

(Note To Self...)

MORE ACTIVITIES TO OPEN YOU TO YOUR PERSONAL MAGIC

The trio that serves your needs (body-mind-spirit) responds well to a daily workout or at least regular recognition. Like athletes or old friends, they are then more able to be there when you really need them! The following is a sampling of some simple ways to stay in touch with the trio. You will add your own as you go through these and as you further uncover what it is that YOU need.

Daily Rituals

Morning

Begin with acknowledging you are awake and alive, even if you feel rotten or have a really hard day ahead. That moment that you first come to consciousness can set the tone for what is ahead.

Greet the day - consciously and with attention to the sun, sky, air and where you are standing/seated.

Stretch and breathe - honor your Body.

During the day

Drink lottsa *real* water.

Evening

Stretch and breathe - honor your Body.

Oils - lavender in the room.

Creative Endeavor

The Arts

If you are already proficient or comfortable in any of the following forms, that can be a useful beginning. However, also stretch into an area with which you are less familiar. Sometimes the form in which we have done the most is also the form that has taken up residence in our intellectual and/or critical mind. This is about *play*. Be sure that you can play with your familiar form with a child-like wonder, without expectation of outcome or critical judgment. If not, do something else!

The ready-to-go Arts 'tool kit'

This should be a container where everything is in one place, so you can delve into it anytime and find what you need/want to play with. Nothing takes the steam out of creative impulse faster than having to search for things and then the things are blunt, empty or don't work! Your basic supplies are:

      crayons

      colored pencils and sharpener

      blank paper & colored paper

      scissors

      glue

      tape

      glitter

      stickers

CDs & something to play them on that works easily!

an aromatic candle & matches

Add to this as you go - you will know what to put in it. Keep it replenished. AND this is YOURS! Please don't share it! Have another place and collection of arts stuff for everyone else.

Generally

When you do these exercises think of them more as explorations and warm-ups, rather than Projects. Do them in the spirit of discovery, wonder, impulsiveness like small children. You do not need to aim for a certain outcome, of a particular level that will be judged. These are for you.

Write

[an introductory word about The Wild Child, who is at the heart of the Performing Wellness™ process and a very useful creative partner to cultivate!

The wild child is not a child so much as that aspect of you that is curious, uninhibited, willing to try anything, say anything, go anywhere. He/she is uncritical, doesn't care what anyone thinks, is always sure and right and can change his/her mind at the drop of a hat and that is OK!]

Dialogue with an Object (from Performing Wellness™)

In your minds' eye, look around your house, garden or anywhere where you are comfortable. Find an object that knows you well - something that you spend time with everyday. I use my coffee pot as it is the first thing I encounter any given day. It could be a hammock, a favorite tree. It needs to be something that you like and that likes you. Something

that is also truthful and honest with you. A kind of
Guardian Angel, Higher Self, alter ego, however you see it.
Start a conversation. Set it up on the page as dialogue.
Your name first (unless it speaks first)

Name: xxx xxxxx xxx xxxx xxxxx!
      (when you are done, a new line)
Object (coffee pot): Xxxxxx!! xx.
Name: *and your reply etc*

Just go with this. Don't think too much. Listen and write
whatever comes - wild child! Soon you will have a real
conversation. Write forward, don't stop and look back.
You have no control over this as we don't in real life.
Write for 20 minutes.

Now read over it! Only make corrections in order to be
able to read it easily out loud, no clever editing please!
And then read it out loud! Hear the characters.

Try some more dialogue writing with other objects in your
house, at work or elsewhere that you know well. It may be
a less friendly one, perhaps pick one that does not like you
or that you don't like and see what happens.

Music Writing (from Performing Wellness™)
You will need 2 different pieces of Instrumental music
ready to play, preferably music with which you are not
familiar and that has no emotional connection. I usually
use a SKY piece called *El Cielo* (Spanish influence) and a

majestic/regal Handle piece. (*Arrival of the Queen of Sheba*)

They should not be too long - about 4-5 minutes each

And as always - the wild child is the writer here!

Listen to the first, without writing. Notice any images of color, shape, movement.

Listen again, writing as you listen.

If you wish, you can write one more 3 minutes in silence or one more with the music.

Listen to the second piece of music - as above.

Note the date on each piece of writing.

Add color to the words themselves. It may be line by line, in sections, around the edges or over the top.

Self as Art Work (*from Performing Wellness™*)

Imagine you are a painting on the wall or a piece of 3-D sculpture. Focus on your inner landscape, not your physical outside. It may be emotional, spiritual or something else and describe that on paper as if you were telling someone on a phone about this painting/piece of art. Write for about 10-15 minutes.

Start with: I just got this new piece of art......

End with: And I am going to put it...

(and say where, eg. the garden, living room, whatever)

Now, look back over what you have written and notice the following:

How many times have you

       used colors in your description

       texture(sharp, prickly, soft etc)

       shapes (square, round)

       images/metaphors (like a river, volcano)

Go back and add to the description, just as it comes to you when you are reading with each of these areas in mind. Add them into the writing or just make lists underneath the body of writing.

Now, with your colors and art collage tools, create this visually as well. Resist the urge to be too real and let it come out fast and messy - find color, shape and movement rather than precision.

Visual Arts

Draw or color. Abstract art is often a great way to play.
Collage.
Clay
Mask making

Music

Create a CD of your favorite music.
Play a musical instrument, not to learn a piece or scales, but to improvise - put the play back in play.

Dance

This is not just stretching and bending but includes the element of free form movement/dance. This doesn't have to terrify you! If it is less formidable, simply call it movement.

Other

- Garden
- Sew
- Cook

GIVE something each day

Manifest your connection to the greater whole.

Examples:

put seed out for the birds, donate a book to an organization, volunteer at a retirement center, make a cake for your neighbor, sign a petition for a cause in which you believe, donate to a nonprofit of your choice, write your blog, water the garden etc.

The list is endless the acts can be big or small, connect with people, creatures or land, private or public. Simply, give something each day.

(Note To Self...)

CHAPTER SIX - YOUR PERSONAL MAGIC OUT IN THE WORLD

THE JOURNEY THUS FAR

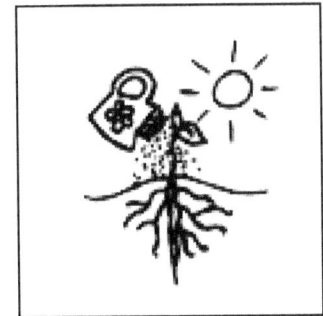

You have arrived here - in this moment. You have made an enlightening journey into *your* Personal Magic, and now what do you do with it? Well of course you already know because it is yours! However, in the interest of completing this book, I offer a final chapter. Refer to it more as the cheer squad, the open hands of invitation and experience, ideas bouncing about for you to then seize as your own, and create new ones.

I will begin with a very, very brief summary of the highlights of the hike that got you here.

Your Soul is the gateway between your mind/body and Spirit/ /God/ /Creator/Power from which we all emanate and in which we all ultimately live. We are each a vital and inalienable part of the Universe in which we live.

Your Personal Magic is your unique expression of that relationship. The creative endeavor, like the wide variety of meditative and prayerful techniques, is a means of accessing Higher Consciousness or Awareness, directly connecting with Spirit.

PERSONAL MAGIC

The Shamanic paradigm reaches back through history to a time when each of us was our own healer and artist with a direct connection to Spirit. In this sense you can become your own wisdom keeper and also make choices about how and whom you call upon for guidance, healing, support and knowledge.

Magic IS real.

• We see its outcome in behavior.

• We feel it in attitude and perception.

• We know it in our hearts.

• It is unique to each and every individual.

Awareness of Self and Nonattachment allows you to be fully engaged in the world and in your life - the relationships, the stories and the unknowns - without being defined by or swallowed by them. Shifting your focus to one of broad-sighted observation, rather than embattled victim, actually frees you to be more present with the people and community in which you find yourself.

Personal Empowerment arises out of this special place. It requires discipline to evoke and maintain, and it deserves - and indeed only really works - when employed with responsibility. Empowerment is nurtured by your Personal Magic. It is most effective when, rather than pulling stuff in toward you, you send outward engaging the world. (It doesn't matter how you do this; it may be very privately - it is the intention to engage that will increase your power.)

It is this Empowerment which, ultimately, frees you to be the hero in your own story, a freedom without fear and with comfort in the Unknown. Your fear exists because you don't know yourself and are unable to find - or don't know how to find - your Higher Self or Spirit. When you can make that connection, you discover there is nothing to fear. The Unknown is simply an aspect to which you have limited access right now. It is not the endgame.

You become less fearful of aging, dying and even death itself. Your experience and wisdom, earned over both this lifetime and the deeper one that becomes conscious over time, is honored. Your unique Personal Magic is the legacy you create. Your Body as the place where the Mind and Spirit are housed is valued and respected, even as it grows tired and breaks down.

As an empowered individual, you participate in your own healthcare, ultimately making your own choices around your life and death. Your accessed ancient, inner Shaman brings knowledge and confidence to work with professionals and others on your journey through your life and the passage beyond.

Paradoxically, the greatest gift you receive is the power to give, to choose, to receive, to decline. Empowerment is at its most magical and powerful when it is turned outward - the gift you choose to give. And that very empowerment authorizes you to recognize and decline that which you do not want or need or that may do you harm.

The basic tools to reach this place (the how to's) include several steps. One is Letting Go for real: honestly, without attachment, and out of Awareness of Self. This may also mean acknowledging what you gain from *not* letting go, before you really can let go.

Another step requires truly being where you are in your life, its circumstances and its difficulties. Positive Being works when you are able to (again) see and accept your current situation in all its particulars without being defined, paralyzed, buried by that information. You can then make real choices about what to do or not to do in that time and place, while remaining open to any changes that may later become necessary.

Meditation and other forms of spiritual intent assist you in reaching the place where you can actually be in your Higher Consciousness and thus have the viewpoint which will give you greatest knowledge and thus choice.

Practicing the arts as a means to Being, also opens that doorway into Awareness of Self, whether or not the arts are for you a means to make a living as well. Playfully uncover your creation without judgment, but with curiosity and joy, free of emotional attachment. The outcome may not feel 'perfect,' but as a creative exploration of self it IS perfect.

Finally, share the story, creation, gift with someone, somehow. The sharing increases its power, magnifying the magic from its beginnings as your Personal Magic into the power of a gift to others. Personal Magic is just that, something which journeys out into the world beyond self.

_____'s Personal Magic 20

Sifting through this work book and all the additional pages you have created, take this time to look back over all that you have created in collaboration with this book. The writing, the art, the thoughts, the Notes to Self.

On a new page (named Personal Magic 20) note what jumps out to you. Can you see a common thread or threads in your story? Where do you find the greatest surprise, the strongest confirmation?

Using a mix of art and words write yourself a short fairytale beginning with "Once Upon A Time there lived '*your name.*' " and tell this story thus far - the story of you and your Personal Magic.

At the end of this chapter you will write another page to the fairytale.

(Note To Self...)

Circularities

In case you have noticed this (and in case you haven't), there are circularities throughout this journey, because in this sort of work one thing inevitably leads to the very same thing that feeds it. A proves B, and B proves A. Perhaps it is useful to visualize the journey as a spiral staircase, where you hike through the same lands, even as the altitude changes with each turn on the path. So if something seems familiar, if you find yourself thinking, "I heard that before," the truth is you very probably did and that is as it should be. On each cycle through however, you will see it with a slightly different slant, make more and more profound connections and come to experience the pleasant sensation of comfort, of greeting an old friend.

Beginning with physical, tangible, visible behaviors and working up from the root, I name the tree like this.

Spirit

Personal Magic

- Giving

- Choice

Personal Magic

- Empowerment

Nonattachment

Awareness of Self

Personal Magic

- Creative Endeavor

Soul

Personal Magic

Spirit

(Of course you can turn this up the other way and see Spirit as working from the top down through your toes. It doesn't really matter because, ultimately, it is a wondrous affirming circle anyway.)

PERSONAL MAGIC OUT IN THE WORLD

How you go about sharing your Personal Magic is unique to you, and it is likely to be different from year to year, life phase to life phase. As long as you are conscious of your Magic, make choices about it and through it, then the power of the gift is intact for you and for all with whom you interact.

Private Gifting

The ways in which you choose to share you Personal Magic may include:

- care of the physical environment (clearing a trail, picking up rubbish)
- tending a garden of flowers or veggies and fruit
- a birdfeeder in the yard
- feeding your friends and family
- keeping a welcoming home
- maintaining the family record of pictures, birthdays, events and letters
- anonymous gifts of goods or money to that which matters to you
- creating your art and 'giving' it away as you wish

Family – Empowerment and Children

A very powerful way to put your magic into the world is through family and children – and they certainly don't have to be your 'blood.' There are many ways to interact with parents and grandparents, cousins, siblings and children - and anyone else you define as family.

Frankly, it is the children for whom our unique Personal Magic is most needed today.

As adults, our gift and responsibility to children is to offer our healthiest and most Aware Self and Personal Magic as we are uniquely able.

Children are usually recognized as anyone from birth through late teenage years. However, it could be anyone whose age and experience sufficiently delineates their youth and childhood from your lived years and experience. In short, perhaps we are all children, and those of us who find ourselves in relationship with anyone 'younger' than ourselves can assume the role of mentor, teacher guide, parent or friend.

However that works out for you, there are some key aspects to the Personal Magic that you have come to that can be shared by the way you live and the stories you tell.

Role of Parents/Adults

What is the role of parents in the encouragement/development of authentic Empowerment of Self our children? First, it involves being able to truly see and own your personal relationship with Empowerment of Self - to take real responsibility for your own gifts and power.

As long as you look to others (maybe even your children) to supply your sense of worth - or offer gifts as enticement, bribes or deals - then you cannot hope to empower others, let alone yourself. Remember, a true gift is something offered without rules about how it is to be used and without any expectation of return.

No-one empowers another. That is something each person must accomplish for him/herself. However, as parents or teachers, you can (and, in fact, must) seed opportunities for that Empowerment of Self to arise in others.

Those opportunities will vary widely based on age, ability and circumstance. It does mean that you find ways to expand the horizons, broaden the activities and environments, and widen the range of relationships and activities for each individual. Through your efforts others may find ways to attempt, fail, succeed and finally experience the true exhilaration of well-earned pride and the empowerment that struggle and outcome can bring.

When there is no space to take personal responsibility, when no one holds you to account as you are learning to hold yourself to account, you miss a vital and essential experience. When all that you want is simply presented to you, when there is no need for problem-solving, you will not, cannot expand. Every individual grows from doing without or discovering the power that lies in other choices apart from the instant reception of a wanted object or outcome. In short, without those experiences there is no opportunity for uncovering the true Being you are inside.

That Being, the empowered being itself that resides in all of us, can only evolve and shine in the light of being and doing as its own person. Parents have an obligation to offer the space and time for those SELF-discoveries, providing a loving safety net and eventually stepping out of the way of this Empowered Being.

Let the children (however you define them) in your orbit know that practicing discipline and responsibility with patience and love will bring you empowerment. When you are empowered, you can choose and if necessary, can say "No."

The empowered young person is better equipped to resist peer pressure, have enough sense of Self to find his/her way through the dark times and stay alive in the face of seemingly impossible experiences.

Share the arts with youth. Bring the theatre to them, take them to the theatre, let them create theatre. Hand them paper and encourage poetry. Spread out the brushes and water colors. Load them up with colored pencils and crayons and craft paper and glue. Play music and dance with them. Take them on a hike, into your garden or out in a boat on the water. Give them laughter.

Provide the children in your world (no matter how 'old' they may seem to be) the opportunity to truly interact and connect with reality through the earth, a living creature, the weather, by telling their own stories.

Most of all, offer them the time and permission to interact with a living, breathing person - YOU! Bring your Personal Magic to assist in uncovering theirs.

_____'s Personal Magic 21

Take time to travel back and consider this:
Was there an adult in your life who shared their Personal Magic with you and encouraged you into yours? (Even if you didn't know it then, hindsight can sometimes tell us a great deal!)
How did they do it?

Write to that person (even if they are no longer around, write as if they are) and tell them what they gave you and how it has affected you. (This is on a separate page)

As an older person, to someone, how will you bring your Personal Magic to them and open them to discover theirs?

Write to the 'children' you will encounter and offer them that gift. (Yet another new page in your book.)

(Note To Self...)

Community

There is also opportunity for bringing your Personal Magic to your wider community.

The Workplace

Be conscious of how you treat everyone where you work, from the janitor to the CEO, the landscaper to the cafeteria staff, the front desk to the client, your co-worker in the next-door cubicle to the new intern. Recognize the truck driver to the sales rep, welder and cowboy, the teacher and the student, the waitress and the clerk. Celebrate the birthday girl at the noisy table and the solitary reader on the back deck of the cafe.

Consciously choose where and when you speak out, how you handle conflict, criticism, and the needs and fears of others.

Where You Live

Observe the needs in your neighborhood, the street, local school, hospital, church, clubs, sporting groups, arts groups, volunteer service groups. Offer your skills and time in the way that best empowers you as well as them.

Beyond

Some people have as an aspect to expression of their Personal Magic taking it beyond their immediate surrounding. If you are one of those, the same approach applies. No matter your medium, be conscious of your intention. Stay grounded and in your Awareness of Self.

You may be a writer, performer, visual artist in the greater world. Perhaps you offer workshops, engage in public speaking, join Volunteers Abroad, found a company, travel as a journalist, a photographer, historian, zoologist. You might be a philanthropist, a research scientist, or a metaphysical explorer.

No matter your exterior expression, it only puts real power into the world and into your soul when you offer your work with clarity of intention and the truth in your heart. Stay in touch with your Aware Self, practicing responsible discipline and disciplined responsibility.

The wider your influence and the greater your capacity to touch others, then the greater the responsibility. You must undertake and embrace a deep, consistent Awareness Of Self to meet the demands, challenges and rewards of this particular expression of Personal Magic.

RESILIENCE AND THE FUTURE

Resilience can be (simply) understood as the capacity to overcome fear, helplessness and anxiety in the face of great difficulty and challenge, without resorting to violence, escapism or victim-hood. Studies of people who do well, rather than those who do not, have revealed common attributes of well-ness.

One of these is resilience, a normal human quality, not a rare thing for some. It can be learned. The opportunities and skills developed through living in community assist greatly in evolving resilience. A personal relationship/experience of Spirituality also seems to be related to levels of resilience.

Likewise, as medical practice has begun to reconnect the body-spirit again, the link between resilience and the individuals' interaction with their environment became clearer and clearer.

Resilience appears to related to the ability to connect with others and to deal with the present as it is, while taking responsibility for oneself and those immediately in your circle. Ultimately the resilient person has a strong personal Self.

In order to cope with the changes, challenges, difficulties and unknowns ahead of us as human beings on this earth, resilience is a key factor to navigating on that journey. Personal Magic is an expression of - as well as key to - resilience. When you are an empowered individual with the skills to maintain your balance – body-mind-spirit – your resilience becomes a powerful piece in your personal tool-box.

The Digital Age

We live in an age where friends are found and made on the net, and many of our interactions, dialogue and socializing occurs through a medium that precludes direct human touch, sound and visuals. Personal Magic becomes more valuable as well as possibly more elusive.

The plethora of information, the speed at which people, news, trends and rumors fly about, can overload, swamp and otherwise blind, overwhelm and confuse you. That shining, deep-centered Self, the one who can objectively Know and respond, struggles against such a tsunami.

Nonstop stimulation, cutting into your time and space to Simply BE in silence and contemplation, makes it ever more challenging to hear the voice and knowledge within. Personal Magic is just that: Personal. It requires *your* personal self-to-Self attention and care.

Passively receiving all this information and/or quickly passing it on (Tweet, Facebook, whatever) bypasses your creative artist within, that link to your Soul. The greatest challenge in this day and age is to keep that artist alive, to stay open to the Spirit and then to have the courage and confidence to give that back to the world.

Resilience in the face of the digital onslaught depends on a capacity to hear your truth, stand in your center and give it mindfully to the world. Resilience is essential as we move forward into the future. Your Personal Magic is your one truly reliable power in the world. It depends on no one but

yourself to be fulfilled, to shine. It is both a link to the community in which you physically live and a direct lifeline to Spirit.

'Responsible Discipline-Disciplined Responsibility' fully applies here! Make choices about how you utilize the power of the digital age. It can diminish your personal power, making you a footnote, lost in an impersonal digital connection. Or it can work for you, enhancing opportunities to share your Personal Magic.

_____'s Personal Magic 22

RESILIENCE!

Using your own experience, explore the word and the meaning of 'Resilience' as it applies to you.

Create an art piece of it. It may be a one-dimensional drawing or an actual 3-D piece.

Imagine Resilience as a mobile or chimes that sway in the wind, all the swinging strands remaining free and clear of each other, creating a beautiful sound.

Perhaps words dangle, what is the cross bar made of? And what is the music it sings? Make a cd to go with this image.

(Note To Self...)

FEET ON THE GROUND AND FLYING

As I wrote waaaaay back in the Prelude, you can be someone who is resilient, optimistic and kind all while being realistic and in the present world.

You can do this on your own. You don't need a book of tricks, a religion, a guru or a formula. No one becomes a magician by watching magicians. No one can be another person. You *can* be who you are and that is huge when you truly own it, talk it and walk it.

This little book has only been the hand, voice and the cheer squad as you take your journey. Nothing is ever set in stone. Ultimately it is your own two feet that will take you along the path.

The previous pages have offered many avenues into the vastness of your creative spirit. Add these to *your* collection of tools. These have been only examples, ideas, and signposts. None of them will be at all useful if you – YOU - sit on the sidelines. There is no real magic here, just a few games to play and ideas to ponder.

When you embrace your personal heroic story, that is when there will be magic. And that magic will be your magic, the magic of the inspired, powerful, creative sprit that you are. This magic will open the windows and doors and lift the roof itself - revealing, restoring and ever increasing, evolving your Empowerment.

Naturally, it is an ongoing enterprise It never ends. What

you have achieved so far as we co-created this book is only one volume of your story. There will be more 'books' for you to uncover, and you will be able to create and grow forever. This first one has only kick-started your process, revealed a handful of threads that lead excitingly into the (at this time) Unknown. This book offered suggestions on how you might honor and nurture your inner artist, the one within who can lead you into your Soul, opening the door into your true Empowerment.

As I predicted in the Introduction, throughout this book you have had the opportunity to consider the potential for real change into better health and greater well-being at many levels. You have seen how the Personal Magic way of Being can impact your relationship with the following areas:

    • your own lifestyle, personal relationships and work you do

    • illness, death and dying (and thus the healthcare system)

    • your ability to handle stress and cope with whatever changes lie ahead

You have had openings into the arenas of:
    • the spiritual domain
    • the arts and creativity
    • the arts and healthcare

Personal Magic means being able to transmute what you hear, read, see, into your own voice and path. Ultimately this book has been about you and you alone -finding *your* path, your Spirit's quest if you like. My deepest hope is that you have found a clearer sense of purpose, an insight into why you are here. Mostly, however, I wish for you to have begun to uncover the magic that is yours, and only yours, to do and bring into the world.

If you are to rise above mere survival and to thrive in the years to come, you will need to be aware of - and have the courage to manifest - your Personal Magic in the world. I cannot write this too often or strongly enough - you *already are* a powerful, kind, resilient and confident individual with an unique magic to share with the world. Own it! The World needs it!

A Cautionary Word...

Resist the urge to rush in on your white horse and Save People! That is your ego defining how YOU will Make Things Better & Improve Everything. Putting your Personal Magic into the world is about creating the opportunity for others to empower themselves. That is the ultimate gift each of us has to give, and that is how each of us, ultimately, empower ourselves.

Offer the Gift where it is appropriate and let it go if it is not accepted.

Be flexible and in nonattachment, able to see and hear what is really wanted and needed.
You may not immediately know what that is. You may need to wait until you do.

The most powerful Gift you have is the capacity to be present, to listen and to offer support.

So, ground yourself consciously in the earth, through your heart and your body.

Apply your grounded intellect to articulate through language and concepts the deeper knowledge within.

Reach from deep within your Soul/Life Force and through that to Awareness of Spirit. Access the greatest power of all, the Orchestra of the Universe, of which you are an integral and vital member.

Feet on the ground and flying, growing and giving your Personal Magic, may you live your life with power, resilience, hopefulness and ultimately with joy.

_____'s Personal Magic 23

Go back to the Story (Personal Magic 20) and if anywhere you have written the words 'fairytale' cross them out and write 'True Story'.

Complete your story thus far, incorporating art, a sound track etc. At the end write in large, excited letters, TO BE CONTINUED...

This is YOUR book. I encourage you to continue to use it, play with it and explore it. Your Personal Magic just that – personal - but if you ever need a hand or a cheer squad, call on me. I am right here, celebrating your journey and watching you fly!

ABOUT THE AUTHOR

Kate Hawkes has degrees in Education, Counseling and Theatre and has spent all her adult life as a teacher (elementary through highschool, community groups and college); and theatre professional (actress, director, producer, playwright). She is an-arts in healthcare consultant, with The Society for Arts in Healthcare, assisting groups to articulate and bring into being arts programs specifically tailored to meet the needs of healthcare. She created Performing Wellness ™, and has taught workshops throughout the country in a wide variety of settings. She works with veterans, children, teenagers, adults and continues as a director, producer and writer. Kate lives in Central Arizona. When not conducting a workshop, running a rehearsal or at her computer engaged in a myriad of endeavors, she rides her horse through the ancient rocks, up windswept peaks and along streambeds that keep her grounded.

www.wellnesswithkate.com
kate@wellnesswithkate.com

RECOMMENDED READING

These are a few of the many books that have contributed to my story and unfolding articulation of Personal Magic. Most I first read many years go, a couple I just recently discovered. I recommend them as a means by which you may deepen, broaden and enhance your own journey of discovery and understanding to articulate your Personal Magic.

Bayles,David and Orland, Ted, *Art and Fear: Observations on the Perils (and Rewards) of Artmaking*, Image Continuum Press, Santa Cruz, CA & Eugene, R, 1993

Capachhione, Lucia, Ph.D, *The Art of Emotional Healing*, Shambhala, Boston & London, 2006

Cowan, Tom, *Shamanism as A Spiritual Practice for Daily Life*, Crossing Press, CA, 1996

Das, Lama Surya, *Letting Go Of the Personal You Used To Be: Lessons o Change, Loss, and Spiritual Transformation,* Broadway Books, NY, 2003

DeSalvo, Louise, *Writing As A Way Of Healing: How Telling Our Stories Transforms Our Lives*, Beacon Press, Boston,1999

Deveson, Anne, *Resilience*, Allen & Unwyn, Australia, 2003

Elinwood, Ellae, and Lanier, Mary, and Garland Noble, Katie, *Earth Your Sweet Spot,* Confluence Books, 2011

Frankel, Victor, *Man's Search For Meaning*, Beacon Press, Boston, first pub.1959, 2006 Edition

Goleman, Danial, *Emotional Intelligence Why It Can Matter More Than IQ*, Bantam Books, NY, 1995

Progoff, Ira, *At A Journal Workshop: Writing to Access the Power of the Unconscious and Evoke Creative Ability,* Jeremy P. Tarcher,Inc Los Angeles,1975

Rollins, Judy, *Arts Activities For Children At Bedside*, WVSA Arts Connection, 2004

Samuels, Michael and Rockwood Lane, Mary, *Spirit Body Healing: Using Your Mind's Eye to Unlock the Medicine Within*, John Wiley & Sons, NY, 2000

PERSONAL MAGIC

Tolle, Eckhart, *The Power of Now: A Guide to Spiritual Enlightenment,* Namaste
Publishing B.C., Canada and New World Library CA, 1999

Wilbur, Ken, *No Boundary: Eastern and Western Approaches to Personal Growth,*
Shambhala, Boston & London, 1985

Williams, Mark and Penman, Danny, *Mindfulness:An Eight-Week Plan for Finding peace
in A Frantic World*, Piatkus, Great Britain, 2011

ADD TO THE LIST!

MUSIC LIST

These are a few of the pieces that I use in workshops and for myself. I urge you to add your own instrumental favorites to the list.

Adagio - A Windham Hill Collection (any of this!)

George Winston (Forest) - Graceful Ghost

G.F. Handel - The Arrival of the Queen of Sheba

J.S. Bach - Little Suite from the Anna Magdalena Notebook

Mozart - Clarinet Concerto in B flat Major

PATH - An Ambient Journey from Windham Hill

SKY (a band) - El Cielo